ISBN 978-1-943521-83-8

Boyack, Connor, author.
Stanfield, Elijah, illustrator.
Miesner, Jim, editor.
The Tuttle Twins Guide to Beware Your Bias / Connor Boyack.

Cover design by Elijah Stanfield
Edited and typeset by Connor Boyack

Printed in the United States

10 9 8 7 6 5 4 3 2 1

THE TUTTLE TWINS GUIDE TO
BEWARE YOUR BIAS

BY CONNOR BOYACK

The List of
BIASES

When was the last time you changed your mind about something? Was it hard to do?

What about this: when was the last time you changed someone else's mind? Perhaps it was about a decision they made or their opinion on an issue. How successful were you? Did it take awhile?

There are powerful forces standing in the way of us thinking differently: cognitive biases. These are bad ways of thinking that lead our brains down paths that don't really make sense. They make us think irrationally and come to the wrong conclusions.

And boy are these biases popular! They're everywhere and widely used by the media, by politicians, and in almost any debate. Why are they used so often?

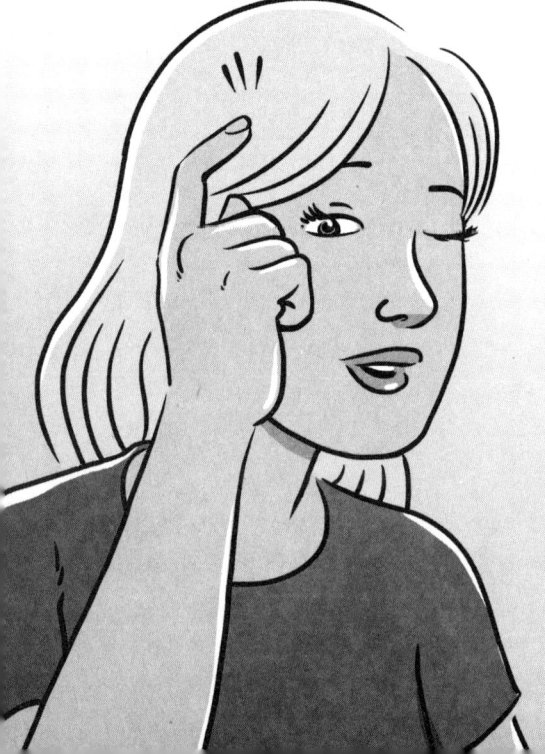

The reason is rather simple: our attention is a limited resource. Our brains are constantly looking for shortcuts instead of having to process information on its own. Instead of fully analyzing something, our brains look for ways to make quicker judgments.

Of course, the problem with this approach is that not all shortcuts are the right route to take. Some lead to dead-ends—or event to disaster. So we should put a little extra energy into thinking things through instead of defaulting to these cognitive biases so often.

That's where this book comes in. Each of these chapters walk you through a cognitive bias so you can understand how it works and how to avoid falling into the mental trap.

Our goal is to help you think critically and clearly so you can find out what's true and not be fooled by the wrong ideas swirling around our society. It's a tough job, but an important one. And we think you're up to the task!

Shall we begin?

—The Tuttle Twins

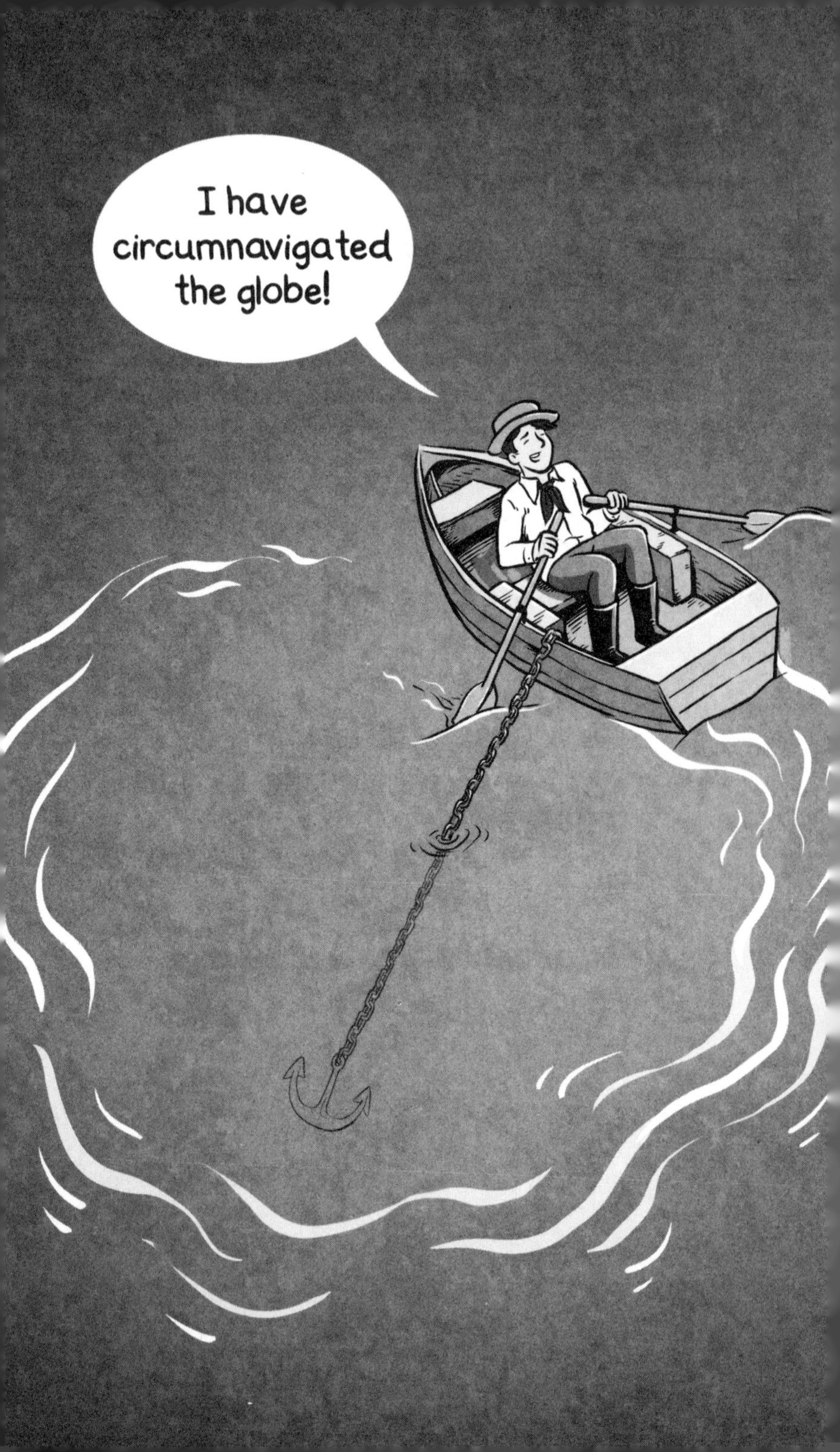
I have circumnavigated the globe!

ANCHORING

When negotiating, the first proposal sets a starting point that heavily influences the final decision. Think independently about how much you personally value a thing and try not to be persuaded into agreeing to something you will later regret.

What a Deal!

Have you ever been in a negotiation with a friend over what to do that evening? What about when your parents bought their last car? Whether it was at a dealership or sold by the owner, they likely had to negotiate. At a dealership, the salesperson may throw out a price at the beginning. Usually, that price is high, and often it is beyond the value of the car. They may add on all kinds of extras that aren't even wanted to justify the inflated price.

Your parents may have no intention of accepting that price, but often it's that first price that sets the tone of the negotiation. Your mom and dad may walk away thinking that they got a great deal because the final price was well below the original offer. In reality, they could actually be paying the car's market value or maybe even a little bit more. Your parents allowed the salesperson's initial offer, or anchor, to affect the price they were willing to agree upon for the car.

Anchoring doesn't happen only at car dealerships, either. It can happen almost anywhere. For instance, say you need a pencil for class because yours broke in your backpack. Your friend happens to have an extra and graciously offers to sell it to you for ten dollars. You may think they're crazy, but you still end up negotiating with them because you need a pencil. After some back and forth, you finally settle on a reasonable price. Maybe you come to the agreement that you will pay a dollar. Compared to ten dollars, that's much more practical. It doesn't seem like you're getting ripped off. But, truthfully, it's still pretty high for a single pencil.

If, however, the negotiation started at a much lower amount, like a dollar, then you'd be less likely to settle on that price. You might end up agreeing on something closer to a quarter as the price of the pencil. The initial anchor makes all the difference. It encourages us to agree to a higher number than we would've if the anchor was lower or didn't exist to begin with.

Marketers also know all about anchoring. By inflating a product's price artificially and having frequent discounts, it can make that product seem like an incredible deal. They know you're more apt to purchase it when you may not have even looked twice at it under normal circumstances. This is why discount chains, coupons, sales, and BOGO offers exist. The original price acts as an anchor in our minds. It gives the item a much higher perceived value than it actually has.

Anchors apply to more than just prices. When a grocery store rations or limits the amount a customer can purchase, that can also act as an anchor. It makes the product appear more valuable and higher in demand than it really is. This creates a scarcity mindset and that affects how many items a customer might purchase in the end. When a store imposes a limit on cans of soup, a customer is more likely to grab more soup than they had initially intended. They may have originally planned on getting only one can of chicken noodle soup but instead walked away with four cans. They allow the limit, or the anchor, to influence their final decision.

Anchoring can affect a lot more than just our purchasing decisions. It can play a role in almost any situation where bargaining is involved or where one party is trying to pull the other party toward a preferred outcome. For instance, it can affect the benefits provided in a job, the stock market, a doctor's diagnosis, and courtroom decisions. Lawyers know this well and use it to their advantage. They may ask for a higher amount in damages or a more severe sentence concerning a crime with the understanding that the anchor will push the judge closer to a more favorable outcome. Sometimes, because of the anchor, the amount that a court awards the plaintiff can be vastly different, even though two people may have almost identical lawsuits.

You even use anchoring yourself. Whenever you bargain with your parents on how many friends you can invite over, the deadline for your chores, how late you can stay up, how much your allowance should be, or how many vegetables you have to eat, anchoring is involved. Anchoring is something that we all use throughout our lives. It's our bargaining tool.

Basically, suggesting a specific value at the outset colors the final decision or judgment. You can think of it as a giant anchor pulling the decision-maker toward an outcome. We may have no intention of agreeing to the anchor. Still, in an effort to be fair and compromise, we're inexorably drawn toward it.

The Anchoring bias usually consists of the following parts:

- Person A presents information X at the outset of a negotiation.

- Person B uses information X in the decision-making process.

- Person B agrees to a final decision based on information X.

An Example with Ethan and Emily

Emily and Ethan were riding their bikes through the park on their way to the library. It was a beautiful, sunny day, without a cloud in the sky. As they were riding, they saw their friend Carlos walking toward them with a large bag in his arms.

"Hey Carlos," Emily waved. "What's going on?"

"Hey guys, check this out." Carlos beamed as he pulled a large red and green dragon kite out of the bag and showed it to Emily and Ethan.

"Wow, that's great," Ethan said. "That bag looks pretty full. What else is in it?"

Carlos pulled out another red and green dragon kite. It was exactly the same as the first. "I got five of them. They're selling them down at the store."

Emily bit her lower lip. "They're nice, but why did you get five of the same exact kite?"

"The store had a big sign that said there's a limit of five per customer, so that's what I got."

Ethan scratched his head and glanced at Emily. "But do you need five kites that are all the same?"

Carlos furrowed his brow. "There was a limit."

"So?" Emily said. "That doesn't mean you need to get the limit."

"Yeah," Ethan said. "It's kind of silly, isn't it?"

Carlos frowned and crammed his kites back into the bag. "You Tuttle twins don't understand a good value when you see one. Whatever. When they're all out of kites, don't come crying to me."

He hurried away, as Emily and Ethan were left staring blankly at each other in confusion.

What Happened?

Carlos allowed his purchasing decision to be affected by anchoring. He may have walked into the store intending only to purchase a single kite, but he changed his mind when he saw that there was a limit. Instead of questioning whether he really needed multiple kites, he decided that the reason behind the limit was that the kites were in high demand, and he needed to purchase more.

He didn't realize that purchasing the same kite multiple times was ridiculous. He thought he had found a great deal until Emily and Ethan questioned him on it. Realizing he had made a mistake, he became upset and hurried away.

It can be pretty common to make these types of mistakes. Sometimes, we can allow a piece of information to color our perception and move us to purchase something we don't even need or want. We might end up feeling foolish, and this can lead to what is called buyer's remorse.

Tuttle Twins Takeaway

Even while being aware of our anchoring bias, we still may fall prey to it. It's hard not to let it draw us in one direction.

There are ways to get around it, though. The best way is by being informed before any negotiation. Understand the value you offer and the value the other party provides as you set your expectations. When you understand something's actual value, you won't be easily influenced by the anchor.

One last thing you can consider doing is to be the first to drop the anchor. Of course, it's always important to be honest and fair and not use this method deceitfully, but it can help you head off any manipulation.

SUNK COST

Don't continue to pour resources into a losing proposition just because of your emotional attachment to the time, money, or energy that was already spent. Once it becomes clear that the outcome is a loss, salvage what you can.

I Can't Quit Now

We naturally want to avoid loss, and when we have a lot invested in something, it can be hard to see clearly. Often, we can end up pouring more time, money, or energy into a losing proposition. You can see this when an investor refuses to sell a dropping stock, or a gambler won't walk away from the table because they've already lost too much.

The sunk cost fallacy can manifest in all sorts of ways. Ever been frustrated with your favorite football team because they keep starting a player that everyone had high hopes for, but continues to make major mistakes? The coaches and owners are affected by the sunk cost fallacy. Likely, they spent an extraordinary amount of money on that player, and they're hoping to recoup some of it through a good performance. It's evident to everyone that's not going to happen, but the coach and owners cannot overcome the bias. They're so focused on the cost that they keep putting that player back in the game and investing more time into them, when in reality, it would be best to put in a cheaper, better-performing player.

A sunk cost doesn't always have to be about money. Think about a boring movie you watched. Maybe you got halfway through and realized it was awful. You didn't enjoy the characters and found the dialogue to be poorly written. But you continue to invest more time because you already devoted a good chunk of it. Many of us have been in that situation. Illogically, we conclude that wasting more of our time makes sense.

Maybe you've played a sport for several years but no longer enjoy it. The logical thing to do would be to not sign up for the next season. Instead, you continue to participate because you already put so much time and energy into the team.

It's also common for teenagers to form groups or cliques. You identify and befriend the people who you think are like you. Sometimes our assumptions are correct and, sometimes, they're false. As a result, we can find ourselves in friendships or relationships that we don't necessarily enjoy. You might even see another group that's more in line with your values, but you don't try to connect because you've already put a lot of time and energy into your current friends.

You can't reclaim a sunk cost. Once you've spent your time, energy, or money, there's no way of getting it back. The most rational thing to do would be to ignore the sunk cost when making your decisions. It's irrelevant, but it isn't easy to see the situation objectively when we've already invested heavily into something. We rationalize that we'll somehow recoup what we lost or make the expense worth it by investing more time, money, or energy.

The sunk cost fallacy typically involves the following parts:

- Person A invests resources into X.

- X is below Person A's expectations.

- Person A continues to invest additional resources into X in the hopes of recouping value.

An Example with Ethan and Emily

Ethan and Emily walked down the street as the smell of funnel cakes wafted through the air, and they could hear the band play in the distance. They were excited. Every year they went with their neighbors Jenna and Tom to the festival in the park to enjoy games, food, and music.

"Bet I'll win another goldfish," Emily said.

"We'll see," Ethan grinned.

They walked up the driveway, and Ethan rang the doorbell. A moment later, Jenna and Tom's mother came to the door.

"Hello, Ethan and Emily." She always had a big smile on her face. "It's nice to see you. Jenna and Tom are in the living room."

Ethan and Emily walked in and found Jenna and her brother Tom playing a video game. Jenna was a green elvish princess, and Tom was a blue mage. They fired at several trolls on the other side of a bridge, clearing them out of the way before they went through a portal.

"Oh, hi guys," Jenna said. "What's up?"

"We were just wondering if you wanted to go down to the fair with us," Emily said.

"Is that today?" Jenna asked as she bit her tongue and fired at another troll. "Yeah, let's go." She hit a couple of buttons on the controller and exited the game.

Tom's fingers danced on the controller. He fired at several more trolls, his eyes fixed on the TV. Several of the trolls fired back simultaneously, and Tom groaned as his character vaporized.

"What about you?" Ethan asked.

Tom glanced over at Ethan and then back to the game as he started at the beginning of the level. "No, thanks."

Jenna put her hands on her hips. "Why not? You love the fair, and you're not exactly enjoying yourself."

"I know, but I've never been to this level before. I can't just walk away from it. We've been playing for too long."

"But if you don't come now, then you're going to miss all the fun," Ethan said.

Tom shrugged his shoulders. "Sorry, I can't. I already have the golden armor. I need to get the helmet."

Jenna waved her brother off and motioned for Ethan and Emily to follow her. The three of them left Tom to play his game. They had a great time at the fair but, later that night as they walked home, Ethan and Emily thought about Tom.

What Happened?

Tom allowed the sunk cost to affect his decision-making. Instead of going out and having fun at the festival as he usually did, he decided to invest more time in a game that he didn't enjoy. By continuing to play, Tom hoped to recoup his investment. He could never get that time back, but he rationalized that the time wouldn't be a waste if he could get a reward.

The truth is that developing a character and increasing skill levels can take hours in many games. If Tom had stopped to think clearly, he would've realized that he and Jenna had been to dozens of levels and collected dozens of items. One wasn't much different from the other, and one accomplishment wasn't any more gratifying than another. Even if he reached the next level or obtained the golden helmet, it wasn't going to make the time he already spent worth it. He would enjoy the fair far more.

This could be an isolated incident for Tom, but the trouble with the sunk cost fallacy is that it's often a cycle. People will throw more time, money, and energy at something, hoping that they will get a return on an investment that never materializes.

Tuttle Twins Takeaway

The sunk cost fallacy can affect business decisions, government projects, gambling, home sales, investments, relationships, as well as something as simple as deciding whether you should continue playing a video game.

When you're not sure if you are being affected by the sunk cost fallacy, try to forget about the past, and separate yourself from the situation. Ask yourself, if I hadn't already invested in this, would I invest now? Is it worth the time, energy, or money? Or could those resources be better allocated elsewhere?

If you're still not sure, seek counsel from those you trust and respect. They might not see it the same way that you do. What's their understanding? Do they see value in continuing to invest? Or should you move in a new direction?

AVAILABILITY HEURISTIC

Memories and information that you can recall quickly seem important to your mind. But the truth might require you to spend more time investigating information that's not immediately apparent.

We're Doomed!

Recent and significant moments in our lives often are the easiest to recall. It makes sense that our minds work this way. If we experience a potentially life-threatening situation, we would want to remember the information quickly so we could avoid that situation again. You might have picked up hundreds of rocks in your life, but you remember the one time a rattlesnake struck at your hand when you did. Now you're wary and don't want to make that same mistake ever again. It's a mental shortcut, in a sense, and it can work in our favor.

The problem, though, is that it doesn't always work in our favor, and it sometimes can be to our detriment. When we value easily recalled information over other information, it skews our perception of the truth and leads us to make incorrect judgments.

You might believe that depression is far more prevalent because of commercials that repeatedly play on TV. Or you might conclude that most Americans identify as Democrats or Republicans, based on recent opinions you heard. (In fact, more people identify as political "independents" than both "Republican" or "Democrat" combined.)

When events are both recent and emotionally impactful, they can act as a double whammy. This is especially prevalent in the news. Reports on a new disease, child abduction, plane crash, or police brutality can heavily influence our perception. Instead of researching and understanding all the relevant data, we make conclusions based on these isolated reports. Essentially, we reason that these issues are far more dangerous and common than they are. This, in turn, leads us to make irrational decisions out of fear.

Take the September 11th World Trade Center attack as an example. After the attack in 2001, the availability bias led many people to believe that driving was safer than flying. Air travel decreased, and instead of flying, more people drove to their destinations. As a result, there was a measurable rise in driving-related fatalities that year. People died who shouldn't have because they allowed their decisions to be influenced by the availability bias.

This bias can heavily influence many judgments in our personal lives, businesses, and even the government. Sometimes, people may say that an issue is politicized. What they might mean is that politicians are basing their decisions on the availability bias and not the facts. Sometimes they do this out of ignorance, and sometimes they are pandering to voters who they believe base their judgments on the availability bias.

The real trouble is that it can be hard to recognize the availability bias, as it is so common and widespread. Even if we're well aware of it, we may arrive at incorrect conclusions because we are not aware that we're relying on it.

The availability bias can consist of the following:

- Person A recalls one (or several) recent, emotional, or unique occurrence(s).

- Person A places a high value of importance on this limited information.

- Person A concludes that a recurrence is far more likely than it actually is.

An Example with Ethan and Emily

Emily, Ethan, and their friend Julia were working on a school assignment. They spent several hours on it and decided to take a break. After grabbing some lunch, they sat down in front of the TV and turned it on.

Ethan flicked through the channels and finally stopped on a commercial where a man was climbing a giant cliff face. He was hundreds of feet up, and Ethan's jaw dropped a little as he watched him climb. The camera panned to reveal the sun setting on the horizon and then pulled back until he was only a speck on the cliff face. Then the screen went black, and the title came up: "Come to Yosemite."

Ethan began to flick back through the channels again. "I would love to do that. Someday, that's going to be me."

Julia choked on her sandwich. "Are you serious? You'll get yourself killed!"

Ethan continued to flip through the channels before he finally stopped on a game show. "It's not as dangerous as you might think. You're far more likely to die in a car accident than you are rock climbing."

Julia took a sip of water. "I don't think that's true. It's super dangerous. I watched this story once where this guy went rock climbing, and both of his ropes broke, and he fell hundreds of feet to his death. Then there was this other time when this girl didn't tie off her brother's rope correctly, and he lost his footing and fell to his death, too."

Emily wiped her mouth. "Julia, those are isolated instances. Around five million people go rock climbing every year, and only 30 of them have fatal accidents. Ethan's right. It's very safe, as long as you're responsible."

Ethan nodded. "You also don't know how inexperienced they were. It sounds like the one guy whose rope broke didn't even have the right equipment. I would also make sure I have a professional guide and the proper tools. I certainly wouldn't trust Emily to tie anything." He smiled, trying to lighten the mood.

Julia took another swig of water and frowned. "You can make fun of me, but it's no laughing matter. Rock climbing equals death. Plain and simple."

Emily looked at Ethan, and Ethan looked at Emily.

"Let's just enjoy our food," Emily said. "I'm starved." She took a huge bite of her sandwich.

The two of them turned to the game show and tried to enjoy the rest of their break. But after taking only a couple more bites, Julia quickly packed up her work and left, claiming she was tired. Stunned, Emily and Ethan watched her go.

"Did I say something wrong?" Ethan asked.

What Happened?

Julia allowed the availability bias to alter her perception of how dangerous rock climbing was. Even after Ethan and Emily told her some statistics about how safe it was, she refused to acknowledge this information.

Instead, she decided to rely on a few stories that she had heard in the news. While the reports were accurate, they weren't a relevant indicator of how safe rock climbing was. The fact that both stories were highly traumatic—resulting in death—left an indelible mark in Julia's mind and created a strong bias against the sport.

Tuttle Twins Takeaway

Part of the problem with the availability bias is that it's so common and easy to overlook that it can go unnoticed. Without self-examination, it causes us to make incorrect judgments and, in turn, bad choices. These choices can impact our family, friends, education, government, economy, and so on.

So how do we deal with it? Try not to form judgments until you have all the information. Realize there are always two sides to a story. Consider others' perspectives. Take time to look at statistics when possible. Do your best to be mindful instead of relying on limited experiences and memories as the basis for your understanding. Just because something is easily recalled doesn't mean that it's an accurate representation of the truth or a good predictor of the future.

CURSE OF KNOWLEDGE

It's a common mistake to assume that things you understand are evident to others. When communicating with others, make sure to consider that they need to learn what you already know.

Easy as Pi

You don't have to be an expert to fall prey to the curse of knowledge. For instance, maybe there's a popular band or singer that you enjoy. You might know all their songs word for word, the history behind them, how they formed, and their entire life story. All of this is common knowledge to you, but when you mention them to your parents, not only are they not familiar with them, but they mispronounce their names.

You're stunned that they can be so clueless. How can they exist in society without knowing about them? Their music is everywhere. It's probably the best music ever created. Have they been living under a rock?

No, they haven't been living under a rock. Their attention was just focused on other things, like their jobs, faith, family, home repairs, taxes, bills, you and your siblings, etc. They might have checked out the group briefly but nowhere near to the level that you did. What, to you, seems like common knowledge isn't actually common at all. You just think everyone knows the information because you've developed expertise in this small area of your life.

The curse of knowledge is most evident in the classroom. As we acquire knowledge, we can forget what it was like to know nothing about a subject. The teacher then might teach from a higher level of learning without relaying the more basic concepts and inadvertently cause their students to struggle.

Maybe you've experienced this yourself. All teachers can slip into it at times—no matter how good they might be, they might inadvertently gloss over foundational concepts necessary to grasp higher-level learning. Or they don't adequately explain the reasoning behind something.

This bias can happen with anything we learn, from bio-chemistry to our knowledge of music and pop culture—something that your parents may or may not be the most current with. Once you know that pi begins with 3.14159, it's hard to remember what it was like not knowing that.

The curse of knowledge is pretty simple:

- Person A learns some new information.

- In time, they forget what it was like not to know this information.

- Person A then assumes everyone either knows what they know or can easily comprehend it.

An Example with Ethan and Emily

Emily and Ethan stood on opposite sides of the gym. Half the group was on Emily's side, and the other half was on Ethan's. This was their favorite time of year. It was dodge-ball season!

Ethan pointed the ball at Emily, and Emily waved her finger at him as she smiled. Coach Murdoch lifted the whistle to his mustache and blew hard. The shrill of the whistle signaled kids to start hurling the foam balls across the court.

Ethan threw his at Emily as she ducked, and the ball slammed into the wall behind her. Finding another ball, she grabbed it and faked a throw at Ethan before blasting another boy in the chest. He didn't have a chance to catch it as it bounced off him and hit another kid in the back.

Running across the court, Ethan grabbed another ball. Using it as a shield, he leaped and dodged several attacks. Snatching up another ball, he used one to block and tossed the other toward his teammate Jerry. Jerry caught it and hurled it at another boy. The ball bounced off his foot, and Emily came out of nowhere, dove, and grabbed it before it hit the ground.

With that, Ethan looked around and saw that much of his team was already out. His team's hope for victory was up to him and one remaining teammate, a girl on the far side of the court. Emily had the advantage with two team members left. Ethan lowered his head in concentration as he formulated a team strategy, and then looked up in horror to see his teammate throw a ball at Emily's team. The throw was high and easily caught.

It was now three against one. Ethan knew just what Emily would do. They gathered the balls on their side of the court and put them into a pile. Ethan ran and grabbed the only one left on his side. They were going to rapid-fire attack him. The best course of action was to stay as far back as possible. The other kids toed the line. Cradling three balls each and another in their throwing hands, Emily raised her arm and dropped it, signaling them to throw.

All Ethan could do was dodge and use his ball as a shield. He ducked and fended off the first attack as his enemies prepared to fire again. This time, one boy was a hair early. Ethan took advantage of the situation, dodged out of the way, and watched as the other two balls went straight for him. Dropping his ball shield to the ground, he timed it perfectly, catching both balls against his chest.

With a smile on her face, Emily threw her hands up into the air. The last remaining teammate stood there in shocked surprise, but Ethan didn't waste a moment. Grabbing the other ball, he spun around and launched it right at his legs. The boy's mistake was trying to catch it as it bounced off his foot and landed on the ground. Ethan's team threw their hands in the air, cheering as they ran out on the court and slapped him on the back.

The coach blew the whistle. "Nice game, Tuttle! Everyone, water break!"

The kids lined up at the fountain and congratulated Ethan some more.

"Wow," Riley said as she smiled. "Those were some moves. It was like I was watching Payan out there."

"Who?" Emily asked.

Riley's jaw dropped. "Payan. Justin Payan? Maybe the best all-time dodgeball player in the WDBF?"

Ethan scratched his head. "What's the WDBF?"

Riley put her hand to her forehead. "You don't know what the WDBF is? You've never heard of the World Dodgeball Federation?"

"No," Ethan said. "There's a World Dodgeball Federation?"

Riley rolled her eyes. "Wow, I have no words."

The teams lined back up on each side of the gym, leaving Ethan and Emily staring at each other before the shrill of

Coach Murdoch's whistle broke their concentration.

"Tuttle twins! Line up!"

What Happened?

Riley's disposition soured as she realized that the Tuttle twins knew nothing about professional dodgeball. She was in shock and disbelief that they could be so oblivious to what she believed was common knowledge.

She had forgotten that only a year ago, she had been in the same situation. If it hadn't been for her brother, a huge WDBF fan, Riley would never have learned anything about it. Through her relationship with him, she was slowly exposed to the league and its many players. Had she taken a moment to remember this, she might have realized that dodgeball trivia isn't common knowledge.

Tuttle Twins Takeaway

When you're teaching, be sure to take your time and assume someone has almost no knowledge of it. At the same time, be careful not to be patronizing.

You'll want to repeat the basic steps or foundational concepts that are necessary to understand the topic. Be patient and allow others time to absorb what you're teaching them. It's also important to remember that the curse of knowledge doesn't apply only to teaching. Anything that we learn can be affected by the curse of knowledge. Don't assume that someone has your level of expertise.

When you find yourself making this error, try to take a step back. Remember, we're all constantly learning throughout our lives. Learning doesn't stop once you get out of school. Sometimes, you'll know more than others, and sometimes you'll know less. Give others the same patience and understanding that you hope they'll have with you when you don't know about a subject.

CONFIRMATION BIAS

Many people dismiss new information that doesn't fit their preconceptions and focus only on ideas that fit what they already believe. Don't distort truth to fit your current view of the world.

Fact Check!

Confirmation bias is sometimes known as the myside bias or the mother-of-all biases. It can be easy to see why. When we're operating under this bias, it's almost impossible to look at anything objectively. Instead, we use our existing beliefs as filters with which we judge new information. Like a mid-1800s pioneer panning for gold, our preconceptions are the sifter. The facts supporting them are the gold, and everything that falls through the sifter is the information that doesn't.

We can also think about it in another way. A good detective starts with clues and builds a case from them, but it's the opposite with the confirmation bias. Confirmation bias is like a detective beginning with a conclusion and tossing out all the clues that don't support it—or only considering the clues that do. We can probably all agree that would be terrible detective work and probably send an innocent person to jail.

Confirmation bias can significantly impact our government, educational system, health care, and courts. Yet, it's most observable in the media as it highlights information that favors its worldview while dismissing contrary information. We also can see this in the social media companies as they fact-check information that opposes their beliefs while ignoring misinformation that favors their views. This can even affect science as the media skews theoretical evidence to appear conclusive—highlighting favorable information while dismissing contrary information.

The late 19th and early 20th centuries are also great examples of confirmation bias in science. During that time, a science called eugenics became popular. Eugenicists believed that they could genetically improve the human race by encouraging certain groups to breed while prohibiting other groups. Through confirmation bias, these scientists came to horrifyingly racist, sexist, and xenophobic conclusions. They essentially believed that certain groups of people were inferior to others.

They even hypothesized that forced sterilization of certain groups of people and selective breeding programs would be beneficial to society. These conclusions, where scientists were led to by confirmation bias, were eventually adopted by some regimes that came to power—most notably the Nazi party—and led to millions of deaths.

We know today how misguided and evil those ideas were. Yet, many scientists and people who believed in eugenics thought they were doing a good thing. Through confirmation bias, the scientists and the people in power in these regimes justified some of the worst evil imaginable. That's why confirmation bias can be so dangerous.

We may never commit heinous attrocites like the eugenicists did, but confirmation bias can affect all of us. Consider the ways that confirmation bias affects our view of the world. For instance, do your parents favor certain news stations or online news sources because of their political views? Are there other sources that they dismiss because of their opposing political views?

People tend to watch news that favors their perspective. Those who lean "left" may watch completely different news stations than those who lean "right." Even if they try to be unbiased, they might still find themselves watching more news sources that confirm their worldview than those that don't. What about you? Is there anything that you favor because it agrees with your beliefs? Or oppose because it challenges those beliefs?

Confirmation bias is strongest regarding the values that we hold most dear. In issues of faith or politics, confirmation bias can play heavily into how we filter information. It can affect our relationships, how we might interact with people, and our opinions of ourselves and others. But it's most dangerous when it involves large groups, industries, or governments.

Confirmation bias works like this:

- Person A forms a belief.

- Person A seeks out and favors information that fits this belief.

- Person A avoids and dismisses information that doesn't fit this belief.

An Example with Ethan and Emily

Ethan ran through the hot sand and dove into the lake with his friend Bill. Kids filled the beach on this sunny, summer day as Emily and her friend Tammy found an empty spot and set up some blankets in the sand.

Ethan ran back out of the water and made his way back to Emily and Tammy. "Ugh, it's still pretty cold. I thought the water would be warmer by now."

"You just have to stay in, and your body will warm up to

it," Emily said. "Anyone want to play frisbee?"

Tammy stared across the beach at a girl in a red bathing suit. "Look who it is."

Emily turned to see that it was Casey, a girl in her history class. "We should go over and say hi."

"She's a cheerleader," Tammy said with disgust.

"So," Ethan said. "What's your point?"

Tammy raised her eyebrows. "Cheerleaders are some of the worst people on the planet. It's a fact."

"That isn't true," Emily said.

"Yes, it is. Have you ever seen a nice or smart cheerleader? No, because they don't exist. They're like unicorns or leprechauns."

Emily and Ethan couldn't help but laugh at Tammy's ridiculous statement.

"What about Diane Sawyer? She was a cheerleader," Emily said. "I'm not sure if she's nice, but you can't say she isn't smart."

"She couldn't have been a cheerleader!" Tammy pulled the sunscreen out, opened it, and rubbed it on her arms.

"It's true," Ethan said. "I remember reading an article with Emily about Diane Sawyer's childhood."

"You Tuttle twins always stick up for each other, don't you?" Tammy snapped. "Even if it's true, that doesn't prove anything."

"What do you mean?" Emily said. "She's a fantastic investigative journalist, and that takes brains."

"I'll prove it to you." Tammy looked around until she saw someone with a phone, stood up, and jogged toward them.

"Where are you going?" Emily asked.

"I'm going to ask if that woman will let me borrow her phone. Give me two minutes, and I bet I can Google all sorts of dumb things that Diane Sawyer said."

Ethan and Emily watch Tammy as she knelt beside the woman, pointed at the phone, and begged her to borrow it.

What Happened?

Tammy was so insistent that cheerleaders aren't smart that, at first, she refused to accept a piece of information that ran contrary to that belief. When Ethan backed up Emily, Tammy was finally willing to admit Diane Sawyer could have been a cheerleader. Yet, she was still unwilling to acknowledge the flaw in her original statement. Instead, she decided that if Diane Sawyer were a cheerleader, then that meant she must be stupid.

With this new line of reasoning, she ran off to prove that Diane Sawyer was dumb, and, therefore, her original claim was still valid. In this example, she both dismissed information that was counter to her point of view and actively sought out information that supported her point of view.

Tuttle Twins Takeaway

Confirmation bias is all around us. It affects how we filter information. It can be hard to separate ourselves from it even when we are aware of it. It can cause us to make biased decisions or cause businesses and governments to implement evil policies and practices that cause great societal harm.

Confirmation bias can also be frustrating to deal with in an argument. When another person is unwilling to get past it, sometimes the best thing you can do is state your case and move on. No matter how much we want to, we can't change everyone's mind.

To guard against confirmation bias in your own life, think of yourself as a software developer, and your beliefs are the beta software. When someone presents an opposing view, take it as an opportunity to look for flaws that need to be corrected. When someone presents new evidence that supports your beliefs, do some research before accepting it as fact. Using false information to support your opinions can be just as harmful as dismissing valid information.

DUNNING-KRUGER EFFECT

People who have a simple view of the world are overconfident in their knowledge. But the more you learn, the more you realize how much you still don't know about the world.

I'm Pretty Much an Expert

The Dunning-Kruger effect is based on an experiment performed by two social psychologists. David Dunning and Justin Kruger concluded from a simple study that those who did poorly on a test overestimated their performance, while those who did well underestimated their performance.

The study makes a lot of sense when we think about it. When you know nothing about a subject, you tend to overestimate your ability. Some may say that it's overconfidence, but it could also be a case of being overly optimistic. With little experience, you might believe that you can accomplish or pick up on something rather quickly or that it's more intuitive than it is.

On the other hand, when you know a subject well, you learn it's more complicated than you first realized. With better awareness of the subject's complexity, you might even assume that there is even more to it, causing you to underestimate your ability.

You might have seen the Dunning-Kruger effect in action at various times in your life. Perhaps your dad can figure out almost any home repair by watching web videos, but when he decided to add a back porch to your house, he soon got in over his head. It's been two years since he started, and it still sits unfinished. He vastly overestimated his abilities. That doesn't mean he's stupid. It just means that he didn't fully understand the level of knowledge required and the time commitment before he started the project.

Or perhaps you've observed this bias in a neighbor. Perhaps it's a friend who entered a baking contest as an inexperienced novice. Or have you ever assumed that you could easily beat a videogame, only to realize it was far more challenging? Before playing it, you grossly overestimated yourself. As time went on, you got better, reached higher levels, and with these challenges, your self-estimate changed. Learning even more about the game, you may have even started to underestimate your ability.

What's essential to remember about the Dunning-Kruger effect is that it's not always a hard and fast rule. Confidence isn't a perfect indicator of someone's expertise or intelligence. Some people might use the Dunning-Kruger effect as a weapon. They may point out that you're confident and, therefore, must be wrong or not intelligent. That's a mistake, and we should never use it that way. Don't base someone's intelligence on their confidence level.

The Dunning-Kruger effect can happen in the following situations:

- Person A studies and learns about a specific subject.

- With increased knowledge, Person A underestimates their mastery.

Or…

- Person B has very little knowledge about a particular subject.

- With minimal understanding, Person B overestimates their mastery.

An Example with Ethan and Emily

Emily helped Ethan push his soapbox car down the street. He had been working on it for months with her help. At first, Emily had made fun of her brother, but she saw how serious he was as time went on. Each night he spent time watching soapbox car racing videos, reading soapbox car sites, looking at past winners' cars, and looking up other obscure soapbox car trivia.

Ethan was hooked, and though sometimes she worried about him, she was happy that race day was finally here. He had shaped one of the most aerodynamic cars that Emily had ever seen, painted it silver, and nicknamed it The Bullet.

"Think you'll win?" Emily asked as they rolled it up onto the sidewalk.

Ethan shrugged his shoulders. "Probably not, but it sure was fun building it, and I can't wait to see how it does."

"I don't see how you can lose," she said.

Ethan smiled but looked nervous as they wheeled it to the top of the hill where the other soapbox car racers waited. No one had a car as smooth and finished as Ethan's. Most were boxes nailed to a frame and likely put together in a single weekend.

As they looked around at the competition, Ethan's friend Brian wheeled up to the line. It was almost hard to tell that his was a soapbox car. It looked more like a pile of garbage, with several different wheels attached. Some of the wheels were bigger than others, and they wobbled as he pushed it. "Hey, Ethan, said your prayers yet? You're going to need them."

"Is that so?" Emily asked as she stared at Brian's Franken-car. It was impossible to look away.

"Yup, I got this one in the bag. My uncle helped me put this together. He won the soapbox car race when he was my age. No way I can lose."

Ethan pressed his lips together and nodded. "It doesn't matter if we win or lose. We're just here to have fun!"

"Keep telling yourself that as you choke on my dust." Brian hopped into his car as one of the side mirrors fell off. He picked it up and tried to stick it back on, but it refused to stay, so he tossed it behind him. "I guess I don't need that part."

"Racers, get ready," a man said as he stepped toward the line with a starting pistol in hand.

Ethan slid into his car, adjusted his helmet, and looked back at Emily one last time before he gave her the thumbs up. She did the same, and Brian's other mirror fell off.

"On your mark, get set!" The man raised the starting pistol, and it went off with a bang.

All the racers leaned forward as their cars began to pick up speed. Ethan quickly took the lead and gradually increased it as the race went on. Brian managed to roll about 20 feet before he careened off the course into a bale of hay, and two of his wheels popped off.

As Ethan rolled down the hill and picked up speed, his

lead increased, and he easily won the race. Emily jumped up and down and cheered him on, but as she looked at Brian and watched him kick his car wheel across the track, she couldn't help but feel bad for him.

What Happened?

While Ethan had spent a significant amount of time learning and understanding the best way to build a soap-box derby car, he soon realized that there was a lot more to it than just sticking some wheels on a box. The people who won put a great deal of effort into making their cars aerodynamic. The more he learned, the better he understood the obstacles to winning and the less confidence he had. This caused him to have a low estimate of his actual abilities.

Brian, on the other hand, put hardly any time into the car. He and his uncle spent maybe a couple of hours building it, from what they found around the garage. With almost no knowledge of what it took to win, Brian grossly overestimated his ability. In the end, he embarrassed himself, as Ethan easily won the race.

Tuttle Twins Takeaway

We need to weigh our understanding of the Dunning-Kruger effect with a certain level of grace. If your friend is confident and passionate about a subject, don't automatically claim Dunning-Kruger and say they're ignorant. And when someone is insecure, don't allow that to make you believe they're an expert.

Ultimately, Dunning-Kruger shows us that confidence isn't a good indicator of intelligence or expertise. We can essentially take confidence out of the equation. That means when considering someone's expertise, we need to do our due diligence and look at the facts. We cannot take anyone's confidence as an indicator that they know what's best. Doing this will go a long way in helping you make better decisions. You won't rely on harmful/misleading advice that appears wise.

Maybe the most significant thing we can take away from Dunning-Kruger, though, is through self-examination. When applying it to ourselves, we should always ask, are we confident because we truly know about the subject? Or do we have very little knowledge about it and are hoping that we'll intuitively understand it?

BELIEF BIAS

It can be difficult to consider ideas that conflict with your existing understanding, but it's important to question your beliefs instead of automatically defending them.

Socialism is all about making sure everyone's needs are met.

That's why I know it will work.

No way. It's dairy that causes cancer.

My uncle drank a glass of milk every day – DEAD at age 38.

Scientists disagree about how the pyramids were built with Egyptian tech.

So, I'm sure it was aliens.

Don't Question Me

Belief bias can be easily confused with confirmation bias. The two are very similar, but they're different. If we put it in simple terms, confirmation bias is about being selective with information, and belief bias is about rationalizing any argument that supports your beliefs.

We can best see how belief bias works when we use something called a syllogism. A syllogism is an argument based on multiple premises. For example, a logical syllogism would be:

All quarterbacks play football. / Billy is a quarterback. / Therefore, Billy plays football.

An example of an illogical syllogism would be:

All rabbits have blood. / I have blood. / Therefore, I am a rabbit.

While this example is ridiculous, it can help to illustrate just how the bias works. We want to protect our beliefs and are more likely to accept an illogical argument if it supports them. Let's change the rabbit syllogism slightly so that it has a more reasonable conclusion. For instance, someone could say:

All rabbits have blood. / Mammals have blood. / Therefore, rabbits are mammals.

Rabbits are indeed mammals. All rational scientists can agree that rabbits are mammals. Since we believe it, we're more willing to accept this argument, even though the logic is faulty. Why is it wrong? Well, many non-mammalian animals have blood, so it's not the characteristic of blood that makes a rabbit a mammal. The argument may have led to the correct conclusion that rabbits are mammals, but it doesn't make the statement logical. We could easily replace a rabbit with an iguana in this example. Iguanas have blood, but they're obviously not mammals.

Sometimes, we want to protect our beliefs so badly that we will accept any argument as supporting evidence. As we've seen in the previous examples, some of these arguments may be valid, and some of them may be invalid. The point is that with the belief bias, we tend to look at the conclusion and ignore the logic behind it.

The belief bias typically has the following parts:

- Person A has a set of beliefs.

- Person A's beliefs are brought into question.

- Person A rationalizes any argument that supports their beliefs—even if the argument is illogical.

An Example with Ethan and Emily

The science fair was in full swing. Ethan and Emily had worked hard on their projects, and the judges had already come around to their tables. Now it was time for their favorite part, walking around the gymnasium and looking at the other projects. Of course, there were always multiple volcanos. This year there were even more than usual. Emily and Ethan had made it a game of keeping count.

"Oh, there's one." Emily pointed. "What's that? My seven to your five?"

"Actually, I have six."

"No, you don't. You have five."

"No, six. Remember the tiny one by the bathroom?"

Emily counted off her fingers. "You're right, my bad. Oh, another one!" Emily pointed.

"Hey guys," Leon said as he walked up to them, holding his science project. "Did I miss anything good?"

"No, Emily and I were just counting the…" Ethan stared at Leon's science project. Inside the box was what looked like a solar system. At the center was a doughnut painted blue and green. "Um, what's that, Leon?"

Leon held it up higher to give Emily and Ethan a better look. "It's my science project." He pointed to the doughnut. "This is the Earth. Over here is the sun. This is the moon, and the rest of these are the other planets."

"What happened to the Earth? Why is it a doughnut? Did your dog eat part of your science project again?"

Leon laughed. "No, of course not. You guys don't believe all that nonsense do you?"

Ethan got closer to the model as he examined it. "What nonsense?"

"You know," Leon lowered his voice to almost a whisper. "The round Earth theory."

"Um, the Earth is round," Emily said.

Leon chuckled to himself. "I expected you Tuttle twins to be better educated than that."

Emily touched the doughnut as it wobbled. "If the Earth isn't round, then how do you explain the spherical shadow of the Earth during a lunar eclipse?"

"Yeah." Ethan touched the transparent moon, trying to figure out if it was glass or plastic. "And how do you explain a ship or the sun slowly disappearing as it goes beyond the horizon?"

"The shadow object and Euclidean geometry," Leon replied.

Emily scrunched up her nose. "What? There is no scientific proof of a shadow object. You're just making that up."

"Yes, there is proof!" Leon said.

Ethan cocked his head. "What is it?"

Leon adjusted the box in his hands. "The lunar eclipse. Emily just mentioned it. That's your evidence. This is real science, and you'd understand it if you just tried."

Ethan rubbed his hand across his face. "What about photos from space?"

"All doctored images. Our government doesn't want you to know the truth. NASA is in on it. Now, if you'll excuse me, I have a science fair to win."

He patted his model and walked away, leaving Emily and Ethan staring blankly. "Did we just slip into an alternate universe?" Ethan asked, wondering what had happened.

What Happened?

Leon's argument was affected by the belief bias. He couldn't support his doughnut conclusion in response to Ethan and

Emily's questions. Without credible evidence to support his beliefs, Leon used any argument at his disposal to defend himself, even though those arguments have insufficient scientific evidence.

Tuttle Twins Takeaway

The belief bias can be far more subtle than in these examples and hard to recognize in ourselves. When our beliefs are under attack, we may feel so desperate to defend them that we grasp for anything that appears to back them up. We must remember to evaluate whether the statements are logical. With our backs against the wall, it isn't hard to see why we might rationalize an illogical argument to defend our views. While the belief bias isn't as common as some of the other biases, it can be a knee-jerk reaction under the right circumstances. Often, it's the bias we fall back on as a last resort.

The important thing the belief bias teaches us is that we have to look beyond the conclusion. Sometimes, we can be so focused on the conclusion that we fail to realize the logic behind the argument is faulty. The most important thing that we can do is look at all the facts to see if they correctly support the conclusion.

It also reminds us that getting to a certain conclusion isn't what is most important. We must discover the *correct* conclusion—and *how* we draw that conclusion is where our focus should be. Using disjointed and irrational logic doesn't help convince anyone you're right. In reality, it's more likely to hurt your cause and push others away than it is to get them to see your point of view (backfire effect).

So how do we keep ourselves from using illogical arguments? One way is not to think in terms of true or false but to consider probability. For instance, the odds that every statement in support of our beliefs is infallible is pretty much zero. Considering this, that means there will be good and bad arguments in support of our beliefs, and it's up to us to discern which are logical and illogical.

We can also examine how we came to our beliefs. What were the circumstances that brought me to believe that this is truthful? Was it because the view is popular? Could it be because it felt right or made me feel good? Or was it because there's evidence to support it?

Another excellent way to combat bias is to admit you don't know everything and come back to an argument later. It's okay to politely acknowledge that you don't have the answers now and ask to return to the discussion once you've reviewed any new information.

SELF-SERVING BIAS

Our pride wants to protect our ego at all costs. Beware of taking too much responsibility for the successes you experience, but also beware of putting blame on others for your own failures.

The Blame Game

Sometimes, when we fail in life, it can be hard to understand why. It's easy to blame external circumstances and more challenging to examine ourselves. This can lead us to decide that something else was the cause of our failure.

When we're successful, it's also easy to attribute it to ourselves. We naturally want to think that we deserve what we have, that we've earned the fruits of our labor. We believe that our strength, willpower, or hard work was the cause and forget that we might be blessed or have some advantage that others don't.

So why is that? Why are we so willing to attribute our failure to external forces while attributing success to ourselves? Shouldn't our reaction to both outcomes be the same? Well, it's pretty simple. Taking responsibility for our mistakes means we have to change, and change is hard. It requires energy and time, while feeling good about ourselves takes almost no effort at all.

We all succumb to this bias at times. And in times like that, the best thing our friends or family can do is to disagree with us. Only when we realize that we're the cause of our problems can we truly fix them and grow as human beings. This isn't the case with the government, though. The government loves to use the self-serving bias against us. Many government programs are based on it.

The belief that there's nothing that you can do to get ahead, that the system is stacked against you, and that you're inherently doomed to fail is the self-serving bias on steroids. While government handouts seem well-intentioned (helping others is good), it's incredibly harmful to those in poverty. It perpetuates the belief that it doesn't matter what choices you make. You'll never be successful, fulfilled, or happy as long as the system is in place (hard work is useless).

Fighting against this bias doesn't mean that we can't be supportive or empathetic when others get discouraged. It's important to listen and allow others to vent without judging them. However, there's a difference between being a good supportive friend and supporting a self-serving attitude. We can help someone without ratifying the idea that others are responsible for their failures in life.

At the same time, we must all realize how blessed we are. If you're reading this, then it's very likely you have far more than many people in this world. Each of us is blessed in ways that many are not. You may not feel that way, but you are. It's best to remember that we all have advantages that others don't.

The self-serving bias can go in two directions:

- Person A fails in some area of their life.

- Person A refuses to accept responsibility and blames the failure on someone or something else.

Or...

- Person A is successful in some area of their life.

- Person A attributes the success to themselves alone.

An Example with Ethan and Emily

Emily and Ethan were excited about summer and all their plans as they tried to concentrate on their end-of-year studies at the kitchen table. Ethan looked up only to see his friend Robbie headed up their sidewalk. Ethan jumped up to meet him and opened the door just as he rang the bell.

Robbie had on a backward baseball cap with a bat slung over his shoulder and tossed Ethan a baseball. "Come on. It's a great day to play."

Ethan looked back at Emily, who was still hard at work at the table. He would love to play, but he wanted to make sure he got all of his work done first.

"Maybe later, Robbie."

Robbie frowned. "Come on, man. It's a great day out. What do you have to do that's so important?"

"I'm finishing up my work. Once it's done, I can play. Have you finished with your schoolwork already?"

Robbie rolled his eyes.

"What's wrong, Robbie?"

"It's Ms. Henderson. She has it in for me."

Ethan remembered Ms. Henderson. She seemed like a nice woman, from what he could remember from his time in public school. She was tough but always fair. "What do you mean she has it in for you?"

"She's an awful teacher. She'll never let me pass. I'll probably end up in summer school."

Emily looked over her shoulder and frowned. "That can't be true. Why would she keep you from passing?"

Robbie raised his eyebrows and shrugged his shoulders. "I have no idea. She just hates me." He turned back to Ethan. "So, are you going to come, or what?"

Ethan glanced back at Emily. "No, I have to finish this up first. It shouldn't take more than an hour. Once I'm done, I'll come and look for you in the park."

Robbie rolled his eyes and turned away. "Whatever."

Ethan closed the door and walked back to the table. He and Emily glanced at each other before getting back to work, but as he tried to focus on his math problems, he couldn't help worry that Robbie wasn't seeing his predicament clearly and that his failure to take responsibilities for his academic struggles was causing bigger problems in his life.

What Happened?

Robbie was in danger of failing due to the self-serving bias. He was locked in a cycle of failure because he continually blamed outside influences, instead of accepting some personal blame and seeking help. Unfortunately, when students have trouble in school, many of them commit this bias. Of all the biases, this one might have the most impact on an individual's education, career, and future. By always blaming others, Robbie is never able to grow, achieve, and become successful. If unchanged, this same bias could lead to a lot of struggles for Robbie down the road.

Failure is inevitable. We all fail. But refusing to accept responsibility only creates a vicious cycle that leads to more and more failure. Blame easily becomes a habit that starts in one area of our lives (e.g., education) and spreads to other areas of our lives (e.g., career, relationships, finances, etc.). To break this habit, we must claim responsibility, get feedback from others, and work hard to overcome our failures. We must look beyond the short-term gain of our goals, too; while achievement is important, our goals are more about helping us develop good habits and discipline that can apply to other areas of our life. Through developing personal responsibility, we can lead a more fulfilling and enriching life.

Tuttle Twins Takeaway

When you fail, it's perfectly normal to look for reasons why. It's okay to look outside of yourself as you try to deduce what went wrong. There are unforeseen obstacles and people who will let you down or try to tear you down. But it's better to make a habit of looking at yourself, because improving yourself is something you can control. This can be difficult. Sometimes, even though we want to self-examine, it can be hard to see clearly. Nothing is more valuable in self-examination than a true friend or someone you respect who's willing to be honest. Get their feedback on the cause of the failure. Was it your fault? How so? Is there anything you could do differently next time? By seeking outside advice from supportive people, you will not only get to the root of the problem more quickly, but also avoid developing unfair prejudices or judgments against others.

When we're successful, we likewise might want to attribute the success to ourselves, but a better habit to instill is the habit of being grateful. Try to find time each day to consider how blessed you are. In what ways do you have an advantage that others don't? (Try to get up five minutes earlier in the morning if you're having trouble finding the time.) As the great scientist Isaac Newton once said, "I stand on the shoulders of giants." Newton meant that many great people came before him—people who made his success possible. Our parents, ancestors, and other great people in history have made sacrifices that make our successes possible.

We must realize that our successes are about so much more than us. There's a far richer and deeper story to them than any of us could ever imagine. You'll probably never know how deep or how rich that story is. Still, in thankfulness, you can appreciate it, and when success comes, place credit where it belongs.

Being thankful may seem like a nice thing to do, but it's about a lot more than that. It centers your perspective and increases your chances of success in the future as you take your ego out of the equation. Going through life with a warped perception of reality won't help you in the long run. There are so many great opportunities available, but you will miss out on most of them if you're foolish or have a negative attitude. Don't lose sight of that. Take responsibility, be thankful, and achieve more than you can ever dream.

BACKFIRE EFFECT

When your convictions are challenged, you might be tempted to dig in your heels and stubbornly maintain your position. Don't let your feelings prevent you from learning the truth.

That Was Unexpected

The backfire effect isn't as common as some of the other biases. Most of the time, we're pretty good at considering opposing information. If our beliefs were to get stronger every time someone gave us conflicting information, then the world would be a much scarier place. It would be hard for us to communicate or get anything done. And society would struggle to function. Thankfully, in most situations, it doesn't lead to us having stronger beliefs.

However, the backfire effect can occur from time to time, especially if we distrust the person challenging our views. When someone shows repeated bias or appears untrustworthy, it can cause us to question anything that comes out of their mouth. If they're aggressive when presenting challenging information, it can make it even worse. Ultimately the effect is our attempt to protect our beliefs against anyone who seems unfair or biased.

If we distrust doctors, we might be less likely to take the medicine they insist we need. If we distrust the government, we might be less likely to fill out a census after seeing advertisements about it. Someone who distrusts the media may find a candidate even more attractive after receiving repeated negativity in the press.

While distrust is more likely to trigger the backfire effect, it isn't always necessary. Sometimes, all we need is for our belief to be strong enough. When we strongly identify with certain views, and others challenge them, it can be hard to separate ourselves from them. As a result, we might feel threatened, which causes us to get upset. These negative emotions make it difficult for us to accept a challenge and that can give our deeply held beliefs an advantage. They act as a shield against opposing evidence.

Also, the more we don't question our beliefs, the stronger they become, and the less likely it is we will examine them in the future. Determination is a wonderful quality to have, but it can quickly become stubbornness if we fail to use reason. What's helpful in one situation can cause us a lot of trouble in another. This is the premise of just about every major movie. A character believes they're right in pursuing something. Through a series of struggles and calamities, the character is forced to reexamine beliefs and change their way of thinking.

The backfire effect typically has the following parts:

- Person A has a belief.

- Person B challenges that belief.

- Person A's belief becomes even stronger.

An Example with Ethan and Emily

The fire felt warm as Ethan bit into a s'more and smiled at Emily, showing the gooey chocolate mess between his teeth. Emily laughed as she turned her marshmallow over in the fire. The stars shone brighter up in the mountains. Though the air was a little crisp, their hoodies, a couple of blankets, and the fire kept them warm.

Two counselors and several of their friends sat around the fire with them. They had been waiting for this time all year long—summer camp. It was that magical time of year when you didn't have to worry about anything. Swimming, hiking, and other fun activities filled your days. Emily twirled her golden brown marshmallow while her friend Samantha's marshmallow glowed like a radioactive isotope.

Emily glanced at her. "Be careful. You're going to lose another one."

"Yeah, I know what I'm doing. I like them charred." Samantha twirled her marshmallow a few more seconds before it slid off the skewer and into the fire. She reached for the bag, but they were all out. "Shoot! Emily, give me yours."

"I'm sorry, what?"

"Give me your marshmallow. I want it."

"No, it's mine. I roasted it perfectly."

Ethan chewed on his s'more as he glanced across the fire to see what was happening.

Samantha pointed at Emily's marshmallow. "You had two, and I only had one. It's only fair."

Emily smiled. "You also dropped two in the fire. It's not my fault you ruined them."

Samantha snorted. "We wouldn't have these problems with socialism."

"Was that a joke?" Ethan asked.

Samantha poked at her flaming marshmallow in the fire. "Capitalism is flawed. It allows an unequal division of resources. Socialism is the more just system."

Ethan took a sip of water, getting the gooey marshmallow from between his teeth so he could talk. "Capitalism may have its flaws, but socialism has failed time and time again. Tens of millions of people died as a result of it. History has shown us that government control of the economy is always dangerous."

Samantha folded her arms. "Denmark, Norway, and Sweden are doing fine with it."

"That's not true. As much as some people want you to believe it, those countries are not socialist. While they have social welfare programs, they do not redistribute wealth. They require all people to pay a good share of taxes," Ethan retorted.

"But they're better off," Samantha quipped as she adjusted herself in her chair.

"No, they're not," Ethan said. "They have higher taxes, lower wages, and pay more for basic goods and services."

Samantha turned red, but Emily couldn't keep her mouth shut. "Even if we significantly raised taxes on the wealthy, it wouldn't be enough to pay for programs socialist politicians want. Taxing the wealthy isn't some magic wand that will automatically make everything better."

Samantha scowled as she looked down at her legs and brushed off the graham cracker crumbs.

Ethan took another swig of water from his canteen. "If we were to redistribute the wealth of the rich, then we would have to do it for everyone, which means an end to owning anything. We would be entirely dependent on the government. All of our rights would be dependent on what they allow. What they decide is good or not good. We would be at their mercy. It would be sanctioned slavery. Not only that—"

Samantha stood up quickly and knocked her chair backward. "Shut up!"

She grabbed her flashlight and headed off toward the girls' cabin. Emily, Ethan, the counselors, and the rest of the campers all looked at each other confused. They tried to laugh it off and make the best of the rest of the night. The next day as Ethan and Emily headed to breakfast, they were shocked to find Samantha wearing a hammer and sickle t-shirt. They thought they had presented the evidence clearly and were left wondering what had happened.

What Happened?

When Ethan and Emily challenged Samantha's belief that socialism was better and fairer than capitalism, she became upset. With her emotions high, Samantha had difficulty separating them from the facts Emily and Ethan presented. She also saw the argument against her values as an attack on her, which made objectivity difficult. In the face of their insistence and unable to separate herself from her views, she stormed off.

As she tried to get to sleep, she mulled over Ethan and Emily's argument. Using emotion and unsupported claims she heard on social media, she refuted their points. Through envisioning this false victory, her conviction that socialism was better became even stronger. Feeling justified, she grabbed a t-shirt that embodied her strengthened belief.

Tuttle Twins Takeaway

The backfire effect can be considered a defense mechanism—a way for us to protect the things we believe. It can be tempting to get right to the point of an argument with statements and facts. However, if the other side sees your approach as aggressive or unfair, you may only be pushing them farther away. Try to take note of this and think in terms of questions instead of statements. Statements have a way of putting people on guard. Simultaneously, questions help us consider information objectively. Statements can be seen as confrontational and create an "us versus them" mindset. In contrast, questions can also bring people together and build cooperation.

Approaching it this way shows humility and helps others see how you came to understand the topic. Instead of telling them why they're wrong, ask questions. Realize that you may be tempted to be sarcastic or condescending, so make sure you're aware of this as you ask questions too.

While it may take more time to ask questions than state facts, it's better to approach sensitive topics this way. Doing so will make it less likely that you'll trigger the backfire effect. Emily and Ethan learned this lesson the hard way.

Just as we can ask others questions, we can also ask them to ourselves. This is called self-examination and helps keep the backfire effect from influencing us. And remember that though it can be challenging to separate yourself from your beliefs, an attack on them isn't an attack on you. Someone's views don't equate to their value as a person.

BARNUM EFFECT

Our minds want to make connections to things, so sometimes we wrongly find specific and personal relevance in nebulous information that holds no direct meaning for us.

It's a Sign!

Our mind is always looking for patterns. We're constantly seeking them out even when we don't realize it. Recognizing them is a crucial part of higher thinking, but sometimes, it can work to our disadvantage. Sometimes, we can see patterns that aren't there, like the face on Mars or a specific shape in a cloud as it moves by.

We usually attribute it to an overactive imagination. However, when we combine this trait with our egos, we have a dangerous recipe. Psychics, magicians, marketers, personality quiz makers, and even some psychiatrists know just how to take advantage of it. Using incomplete information, they can move us toward a conclusion that isn't true.

Have you ever looked at a horoscope before? Horoscopes are generally positive but vague. They're built this way on purpose. Naming a list of favorable qualities strokes your ego and triggers the Barnum effect in your brain. Though we may not even believe in it, we might agree that we have many of the qualities that the horoscope mentions. There's a specific personal connection to it.

What about a personality test? Perhaps you took one on social media recently? It might have asked you some seemingly irrelevant questions about your favorite TV shows. In the process, it told you some of your defining personality traits. As ridiculous as you realize it is for personality to be defined by what television shows you watch, you found it to be surprisingly accurate. This is another example of the Barnum effect in action.

Whenever you get an email from a company with custom recommendations, it's likely that the company is employing the Barnum effect. Generally, a company sends out the same emails to everyone, with just a slight variation based on what you might have ordered in the past. You perceive that they care and are paying attention to you. It feels like you have a connection, and you identify more with the brand. But, in reality, you've just been fooled again by the Barnum effect!

It may feel good to have our egos stroked by a horoscope or receive an email from a company with personalized recommendations. However, what seems real is just incomplete information designed to fool us into believing a lie. The problem with the Barnum effect is that it can feel so real that you fall for it over and over again.

The Barnum effect works like this:

- Person A receives vague (generally positive) information with a declaration that it relates specifically to them.

- Person A interprets the declaration as true and becomes convinced that the information is accurate and specific.

An Example with Ethan and Emily

As they pulled up to their family reunion, Ethan and Emily were excited to see the pavilion in the park, filled with dozens of Tuttles. This was the only time of year when they got to see a lot of their family and most of their cousins.

Emily popped open the car door as they parked, and Ethan did the same. They had been sitting in the car for over two hours and couldn't wait to stretch their legs. Running toward the pavilion, they left their parents behind and saw several of their cousins kicking a soccer ball.

"Hey, Emily and Ethan!" their cousin, Little Joe, yelled as he waved at them.

Ethan and Emily waved back, and one of the older cousins passed the ball to Ethan as they all ran down the field toward the goal. He looked across the field to find Emily open and kicked it toward her. She ran right at the goalie, and with a spectacular kick, blasted it over the goalie's outstreched arms and into the net.

"Nice!" Ethan yelled as he high-fived Emily.

"Nice shot!" Little Joe yelled as he jogged up to them. He was wearing a bright green Hawaii T-shirt and blue camo shorts. "That was incredible. I bet you're a purple monkey. Am I right?"

"Excuse me?" Emily asked.

"You haven't taken that new personality quiz that everyone's taking on social media?" Little Joe asked.

Emily shook her head. "No, I haven't seen it."

Someone whistled, and the rest of the kids ran off the field toward the pavilion where the parents were beginning to pass out hamburgers and hotdogs.

Joe fanned himself with his shirt. "It's a great quiz! You just answer a few questions about your favorite food, color, and birthday, and it'll tell you exactly what kind of person you are."

"Those are a scam," Ethan said. "It's the same concept as horoscopes or palm readers."

Little Joe's eyes got wide. "Oh, no. This is legit. It's 100% accurate. Spot on. I was skeptical at first, but it pegged me."

"What did yours say?" Emily asked.

Little Joe smiled and pulled out his phone. He went to his favorite social media app and showed Emily and Ethan the screen. "I'm a red eagle. See what it says here? You are strong and powerful. You prefer structure over chaos. You have an inner sense of peace that others respect. When necessary, you can make quick decisions and are a natural achiever. Eagles are the leaders of the future. The sky's the limit."

Ethan cleared his throat. "That's real nice, Joe, but that could be anyone. They make those things vague on purpose. Anyone can think of themselves as strong and powerful. I don't mean to burst your bubble, but it's true."

Joe grumbled. "You're just jealous. That sounds like something a blue raccoon would say."

Ethan looked at Emily and shrugged his shoulders. "Okay, who wants to get a burger?"

Ethan and Emily started to make their way toward the line but noticed that Joe wasn't coming with them. When they turned around, he was still standing in the same spot with his head down.

"Hey, Joe!" Ethan yelled. "Want a burger?"

Joe looked at the line. He was no longer smiling. "No, that's alright. I'm not that hungry. I'll meet up with you guys later." Then he turned back around and jogged until he found the soccer ball and kicked it around by himself.

What Happened?

The result of Joe's personality test was a list of positive qualities—just vague enough to apply to anybody. Still, he was proud of it. Of all his friends, he was the only one to get the red eagle. He had often thought he had the potential to be a great leader, but he had never shared that dream with anyone. He had never really led anything in his life, but the test was proof that he could do anything. The sky was the limit. He could be President of the United States if he wanted to.

While it's great to be optimistic about yourself and your goals, Joe built his new identity on a lie. When Emily and Ethan told him that the test was a joke, it was like telling him that his new aspiration was a joke. Dejected, he felt like a fool and wanted to spend some time alone.

Tuttle Twins Takeaway

Marketers, psychics, personality test makers, and others can use the Barnum effect to take advantage of us. We end up believing something that isn't true. While it may seem innocent or not a big deal, it can become a problem.

By allowing the Barnum effect to warp our sense of reality, we can make irrational decisions. Even Myers-Briggs, one of the most popular personality tests worldwide, has little scientific evidence to show that it is accurate. Studies have shown that the test can yield vastly different results depending on the person's mood or the time they take it.

The problem with this is that many people base their career decisions on these types of tests. They may invest a large sum of money and time working toward something they think is their purpose when, in reality, they were led to it more by chance than science.

Also, remember that little things grow into big things. It may seem like fun to believe that horoscopes and personality tests can give you some special insight. The problem is that they subconsciously lead you into making false assumptions about yourself and encourage terrible decision-making. The best and most practical way of avoiding the Barnum effect is to stay away from these tests altogether.

GROUPTHINK

Peer pressure can lead you to adopt opinions and believe ideas that are popular with your social group. Something isn't true just because most people think it is, so take time to evaluate something critically before you form an opinion about it.

Ignorance Is Strength

When we identify with a group, there's always social pressure to conform to that group. This isn't always a bad thing. It can aid in creating a common moral code. For example, our parents taught us that stealing and hitting people was wrong. We want to be accepted, so we conform to the group (i.e., society).

We don't question these fundamental morals as we grow; we simply adopt them as they are consistently reinforced by people we know and trust. While not stealing or hurting each other is mutually beneficial, groupthink is different. It leads to terrible judgments that are harmful and have disastrous results.

In a way, peer pressure can be considered a common example of groupthink. The group pressures you to change your behavior to fit the norm. Whether this pressure comes from a friend or someone else, we're coerced into conforming to the group rather than retaining our individuality. Resistance is seen as an act of hostility as the group increases pressure on the individual.

Groupthink flourishes when a group is isolated. This can result from physical isolation or when a digital platform becomes hostile to opposing opinions. With group members unable to access other viewpoints, they begin to feel a false sense of unity as everyone agrees. In this environment, highly biased leaders can quickly rise and push the group toward poor decisions even faster, resulting in catastrophic effects.

Many examples of this type of behavior can be seen throughout history: communism, fascism, the Salem witch trials, the Spanish Inquisition, the French Revolution, McCarthyism, and the Chinese Cultural Revolution are all examples of groupthink at its worst. Our worst moments in history happen when individuals fail to question the group they belong to—whether they believe in the message or just fear being attacked for not believing it.

No area in society is immune to groupthink, be it business, politics, science, medicine, government, religion, or the media. Groupthink can make us close-minded, irrational, complacent, overconfident, naive, ignorant, and blindly obedient. Of all the biases in this guide, it may be the most dangerous. With the power of numbers, poor decisions are magnified on a national or worldwide scale.

Even when some group members realize how dangerous or misguided a group is, it can easily get out of control and be almost impossible to stop. If a group member questions the group's motives, they can be attacked, demonized, and destroyed.

Groupthink can also cause people to act irrationally or out of character and do things they would never have considered on their own. Led by fear of disagreeing with the group or the conviction that the group is morally right, terrible acts are possible.

The process of groupthink is more complicated than the other biases and often consists of the following:

- Members of the group strongly believe that the group is morally right (or on the right side of history).

- Individuals believe the group is invincible as long as everyone acts together.

- Group norms dismiss any need for analysis of their actions and empahsize the justification of group behavior as correct since their cause is correct.

- Pressure within the group promotes self-censorship, rejection of criticism, an illusion of unanimity, and reporting of any dissent.

- Group members tend to stereotype people who don't belong to the group.

An Example with Ethan and Emily

One beautiful Saturday morning, Emily and Ethan decided to earn some extra money by washing the family car. Ethan sprayed down the van as Emily scrubbed it with a soapy sponge. Out of the corner of his eye, Ethan noticed his neighbor Fred's house. His jaw dropped as he froze in place, and the hose dropped from his hand.

Emily looked up in surprise. "What is it?"

Ethan pointed toward Fred's house, and Emily stood up to get a better view. Someone had ripped the American flag off the house and spray-painted letters across Fred's porch. Emily dropped the sponge, and they both ran over to check on Fred. On the ground, Ethan found a spray can, a bent yard sign, and a torn American flag. He picked up the flag as Emily ran up the porch and rang the doorbell.

A moment later, Fred was at the door. "Hello, Emily. How are…" Fred looked past her to see Ethan holding the flag. He stepped out on the porch and surveyed the damage. Shaking his head sadly, he took the flag from Ethan. "Are you two okay? Is anyone hurt?"

"We're all fine," Ethan said. "We just noticed this while we were washing the car."

"Come in," Fred said as he waved them inside.

"Are you going to call the police?" Emily asked.

"I'll file a report, but it was probably just some kids." He shook his head again. "I can paint over the graffiti, put up a new flag, and get a new sign. The real problem is where all of this is going."

"What do you mean?" Emily asked.

"They targeted me because of the flag and veteran sign in my yard. I never thought I would see this in my lifetime."

"See what?" Ethan asked.

Fred stared him straight in the eyes. "Do you know what groupthink is?"

"Mom taught us about it," Emily said. "That's when a group's beliefs override rational thought and behavior."

Fred smiled. "Excellent, Emily. Sometimes groupthink can be relatively harmless, like when we all believe our last-place football team will go to the championship. Other times, it's used to target and attack specific people based on race, religion, class, or beliefs. That's what the Nazis and Communists did when they rose to power."

"I'm glad to live in a democratic republic. We don't have to worry about that," Ethan said proudly. "We have a Constitution and checks and balances to guard against abuses of power."

"I don't mean to burst your bubble, Ethan, but groupthink

doesn't respect borders or checks and balances. A man named Edmund Burke once said, 'The only thing necessary for the triumph of evil is for good men to do nothing.'"

"Those letters in the graffiti," Emily said. "I've seen them before. Some of my friends have yard signs with them. I heard other kids are changing their social media profiles to that group's symbol. It's like that's all they care about."

Ethan nodded. "Yeah, I don't recognize some of my friends anymore. They're obsessed with this new cause. It's like a religion."

Fred motioned for Emily and Ethan to take a seat. Fred sat across from them and began delicately folding the flag on his lap. "You're right, Ethan. That's exactly what groupthink is. It's a religion."

"How can it be a religion if it doesn't believe in God?" Emily asked.

Fred smiled again. "You don't need to believe in God to be religious. All you need is to be faithfully devoted to a cause above all else." He finished folding the flag and set it aside. "You see, we all need a mission, Emily. God made us to seek a purpose greater than ourselves. Groupthink capitalizes on this. People in a group believe they're doing something noble. For many, this is the first time they felt real purpose. It's exciting." He looked down at the flag. "As evil as the Nazis and Communists were, they couldn't accomplish their goals without support. Many people who supported them thought they were doing something good. They convinced themselves they were on the right side of history. They didn't realize how easily a cause can be perverted until it was too late."

He set the flag on a side table and reached into its drawer. Fred pulled out a small locket, popped it open, and handed it to Emily. Emily looked down at the image of a young girl inside.

Fred cleared his throat. "That was my mother's cousin. They were pen pals. She was about your age when the Nazis brought her family to a death camp. I know you believe nothing like that could ever happen here. Still, it's a reminder to me that when we're complacent and don't stand up for what is right, incredible evil is possible."

Ethan and Emily both stared at the locket, at a loss for words. Could something that horrible ever really happen here?

What Happened?

Ethan, Emily, and Fred never saw who committed the vandalism to his home. However, it was evident by the graffiti that Fred was targeted because of his beliefs. The people who committed the crime wanted to intimidate Fred into silence. This is one of the trademarks of groupthink. Group members hope that their intimidation will force others to self-censor. Through self-censorship, they're able to claim the illusion of unanimity.

While this didn't work on Fred because he would repaint the house and get a new flag and sign, it can be an effective tactic. Fred taught Ethan and Emily that while conforming to the crowd or being silent may be the easy thing to do, that doesn't mean it's the right thing to do. Groupthink can happen anywhere, and we can't allow ourselves to grow complacent or silent out of self-interest. Because when good people refuse to stand up, nothing is left to stand in the way of evil.

Tuttle Twins Takeaway

The critical thing to remember about groupthink is that unity doesn't mean the group's decision is correct or moral. As we've seen in history, groupthink can lead to behavior that individual group members would never consider on their own.

If you're in a leadership role, there are some things you can do to combat groupthink. Give others time to come up with solutions to the problem you face before sharing yours. Also, assign at least one person to the role of devil's advocate for anything that the group might come up with. Finally, discuss the group's decision with an outsider and encourage group members to be critical of the final decision.

However, if you're not a leader, avoiding groupthink is more complicated, especially when you find yourself in the midst of it. Going against the grain is never easy, but we can still develop a habit of asking questions and not allowing popular opinion to lead us. Remember, the greatest heroes in history were willing to stand up against groupthink no matter the personal cost. Sometimes, we believe heroes are remarkable in some way and different from us. Yet, Rosa Parks, Dietrich Bonhoeffer, Susan B. Anthony, and Frederick Douglas were all just regular people willing to stand against groupthink.

NEGATIVITY BIAS

Thinking negatively about something can color your perspective in an unhelpful way. Don't let your pain or problems distort the truth.

I'm Sorry to Hear That

We tend to remember the bad things that happen more than we do the good things. As a result, we can place more importance on negative experiences, letting them have too much influence in shaping our mindset. This explains why if you are having a great day, sometimes, all it takes is one bad thing to ruin it. Or maybe something negative happened to you a long time ago (e.g., an insult, rejection, or personal failure). Whenever you're in a similar situation, it immediately comes to mind. You can't forget it! Both phenomena result from the negativity bias, but the real danger is that it skews reality and leads us to make decisions based on false assumptions.

Have you ever said something silly that others made fun of, and you were less likely to speak up the next time? Or stumbled over your feet in a crucial moment in a basketball game and then decided not to try out for the team the following year? Maybe you did awful on a few math tests (that you didn't study for), and now you hyperventilate at the mere mention of one. All of these situations are examples of the negativity bias's influence in your life. It heavily weighs down your beliefs which affects your future decisions.

Sometimes, it can be hard to get away from negativity, even when we're aware of it. Anyone who's watched any news broadcast for more than thirty seconds knows this to be true. That's because negative news receives more attention, causing a great abundance of these types of stories. The negativity bias dominates the news cycles, but it also permeates politics and social media. Negativity is, unfortunately, a part of our world. Often, the only solution seems to be to turn off the screens, but you still might not be able to get away from it. We all know someone who's always negative. Every time you see them, they're down about something. You try to be upbeat, but they're always negative, without fail. It's like they don't realize that plenty of good exists in the world too. Have they forgotten how to be positive?

This is one of the most significant side effects of the negativity bias. It can lead to a very self-centered perspective. We become so focused on our problems that we lose sight of everything else. We might harp on a flat bike tire and fail to realize our friend just lost a relative. As human beings, we're made to live together, work together, and solve each other's problems. There's nothing more fulfilling than helping others, but the negativity bias keeps us from seeing things clearly. This can stop us from serving others effectively, living up to our true potential, and finding personal fulfillment.

Don't be too hard on yourself, though, if you have trouble with negativity. There isn't a single person in the world who hasn't been negative at some point. Often, we tend to avoid examining negative thoughts because we don't want to think about them. We can form beliefs about ourselves or others that go unchecked because of this. If someone manages to challenge us, we may gloss over the subject or deflect the challenge which keeps us from ever really dealing with the issue at hand.

This isn't a psychology book, but it's important to understand just how deeply this bias can affect us. Even when we're aware of it and examine ourselves routinely, we can still fail to recognize areas in our lives affected by the negativity bias.

The negativity bias can consist of:

- Person A has a negative experience or receives negative information.

- Person A dwells on or remembers the negative more than the positive.

- Person A allows this lopsided understanding to disproportionately influence their attitude and decision-making.

An Example with Ethan and Emily

Ethan stepped back to survey the kitchen counter. He had collected all the ingredients to make his mom's special Super-Mega-Double-Chocolate Brownies. He lowered the scoop into the flour canister just as Emily walked into the room.

"Want to help?" he asked. "I'm making Mom's Super-Mega-Double-Chocolate Brownies."

Emily smiled. "No, thank you. I'm busy."

"You just finished a movie and it's winter break. What do you have to do?"

Emily glanced at the ingredients. "I just don't want to."

Ethan put his arm around her and playfully pulled her toward the bowl. "Come on. It'll be fun."

Emily jerked her body away. "Let go of me. I said no."

Ethan looked at her, confused. "What's wrong? Why are you upset?"

"I'm not good at cooking, okay? I'll screw it up."

Ethan laughed, wondering if this were a joke. "How can you say that? We've cooked together dozens of times, and our food almost always turns out great!"

Emily frowned. "Every time I try to bake, it's a disaster. Remember when we tried to make Dad's birthday cake?"

"Oh yeah, you used the wrong kind of flour."

"And Dad's cake exploded all over the oven."

Ethan couldn't hold back a smirk. The house smelled like burnt chocolate for weeks.

Emily sighed. "Or that time I used salt instead of sugar for the muffins."

Ethan coughed as he remembered the super salty muffins. "They were a little different."

"I'm just an awful baker. I'll screw it up."

"Come on, Emily. That was two times. Are you going to give up over two mistakes? What about the time you made Mom's birthday cake or when we made cookies for the church bake sale?" Ethan reached out his hand. Emily stepped back, throwing up her hands.

She looked at the door behind her. "I've screwed up way more than that, but I don't feel like detailing all of them for you today. You'll have to do this one on your own. Sorry, Ethan," Emily said as she left the kitchen.

What Happened?

Emily had only negative memories about cooking. Though Ethan tried to reassure her that she had succeeded other times, the strongest memories that she had of cooking were negative. Due to these negative associations, Emily had formed an incorrect perception of herself, namely that she was a lousy baker. The negative associations were so strong that she couldn't get past this insecurity, leaving Ethan to bake the brownies all by himself.

Tuttle Twins Takeaway

When you catch yourself being negative, try to evaluate problems in terms of probability. For instance, instead of believing you'll fail, ask yourself what the odds are that you'll succeed. If the odds don't seem good, then ask what you can do to increase them. Try to also counter those thoughts by remembering all the positives. There are multiple ways you can do this. A pros and cons list, or pluses and minuses list, can be a good way of helping you be objective about any decision. It forces you to think of the positives as well as the negatives.

While a list can help you make a decision, it can also help to cultivate thankfulness in prayer or time alone. Odds are that you're better off that most people in the world. Spending a little time each day focusing on what you're grateful for can help clarify your perspective and combat negativity. It's also crucial to understand that many of the things we believe about ourselves aren't true, but formed in our minds because of the negativity bias. Again, this isn't supposed to be some self-help pep talk. It's just a fact.

DECLINISM

Your poor memory will lead you to overstate how good things were in the past—and you'll also likely expect the future to be worse than it actually will be.

Kids these days have no respect.

Back in my day, we obeyed our parents and civil authorities. We did what we were told.

The economic crash proves it.

The best times are behind us. Our world will never be as free and prosperous again.

Entertainment is awful these days.

So much violence and profanity, not like in the 80s —the height of wholesomeness.

COMETS
70

It's the End of the World

As we grow, we look back on the past fondly and remember it better than it was. In difficult times, this happens even more as we look to the past as a form of escape. By simple logic, we then see the past as better than the present and anticipate the future to be even worse.

This may primarily be the result of something called the reminiscence bump. Between the ages of 10 and 30, we naturally experience ever-increasing amounts of independence. When we reminisce, we look back on this period of our life with rose-colored glasses and a sense of fondness. Those years may, in fact, have been great for us, but we mistakenly attribute the good memories to the general condition of the world at that time instead of the fact that they happened during a specific period in our lives, which causes us to misperceive the past. This, in turn, contributes to us drawing incorrect conclusions about the present and future.

You don't have to be older to fall under declinism, though. It can affect kids as well. Maybe you remember when school was easier. Tests weren't as hard. You didn't have many of the problems that you do now. Kindergarten was all about naps, snacks, art, and gym. You reminisce and decide that life was easier then. Comparing it to the present (when homework and tests are common), you assume that school will only become more painful. That's declinism. It's also a lie.

In the process, you forgot about many of the struggles that you had in elementary school. You forgot how difficult it was to make new friends. You forgot the stress of being away from your parents for the first time or trying to figure out a whole new way of doing things. Besides that, you forgot there are many fun things you enjoy now that you didn't get to do then. You didn't have many of the subjects you love or the same level of freedom and independence.

Declinism is influenced not only by our faulty recollections but also by watching too much news or consuming too much social media. Because of the negativity bias (declinism's partner in crime), we naturally fixate on the negative things that happen. Our brain seeks a form of escape, and we look back on fonder times (when the world was nice and cozy). From there, it isn't hard for us to determine that society is in decline and will worsen as time goes on.

Declinism can also become a self-fulfilling prophecy. That means we could conclude there is nothing we can do to stop the decline. We presume it is inevitable, and we act in a way that makes our predictions come true. With all of this in mind, declinism isn't always a bad thing. It can help us realize when we're going in the wrong direction, consider alternative options, and change course before it's too late.

Declinism usually involves the following:

- Person A reminiscences about good memories of the past.

- Person A compares the past to the present.

- Person A believes we're in a state of decline and predicts the future will be even worse (than it probably will be).

An Example with Ethan and Emily

Ethan nodded his head to the music as he looked around the party, and Emily set Tommy's birthday present down on a table. They were in the middle of grabbing some punch just as the lights in one of the rooms flicked off, followed by the music.

"Did the power go out?" someone yelled.

A moment later, Tommy's mom flicked the lights back on as Tommy's sister Katie stood next to the silent Bluetooth speaker.

"Please stop doing that," their mother said.

"Mom, if we're going to save the planet, we need to conserve energy," Katie whined.

"Katie, how many times do I have to tell you? Let your brother enjoy his birthday party." She looked around the room. "How about we open presents?"

Someone handed Tommy a present, and Katie grabbed hold of it. "Let's not tear it open like an animal, Tommy. We can reuse the paper and save the trees." Carefully and slowly, Katie opened the wrapping paper without tearing it.

Exasperated, one of the guests called out, "Katie! What's wrong with you?"

"I'm sorry if I'm the only one who cares about the planet, but if each of us doesn't do our part, then we'll all be dead in ten years."

"Is that true?" Tommy asked, worried.

"That's not true," their mom said, taking the present from Katie and handing it to the birthday boy. "You're scaring your brother, Katie."

"The world is falling apart, Mom. Look at the wildfires in California. If we don't ban cars soon, then our whole world will be on fire."

"Who wants cake?" Katie's mom half-smiled and made her way back into the kitchen.

Ethan scratched his head. "Where are you getting this information from, Katie?"

"I don't have to get it from anywhere. I know it. There weren't as many wildfires when we were kids. There was more polar ice, and the polar bears weren't on the verge of extinction."

Ethan shook his head back and forth. "Polar bears are not on the verge of extinction, Katie. Their numbers are thriving more than ever, and the polar ice is growing, not shrinking. Also, forest fires have nothing to do with global warming. If heat were necessary for forest fires, then we would see more fires near the equator. And that simply isn't the case. The increased prevalence of forest fires has to do with the failure to manage our forests properly, not global warming."

Katie scoffed. "You're one of those climate change deniers."

"No need to resort to name-calling. I'm not a climate change denier. The climate is constantly changing, and I don't deny that humans may affect it. But we need to consider all of the evidence before we panic. If we act irrationally based on limited data, that could have even worse consequences."

"I misspoke. You're not a climate change denier. You're a science denier."

Emily flushed red and stepped forward to defend her brother. "All Ethan is doing is questioning your prediction. Questions are the cornerstone of science. Using intimidation to silence people is exactly what they did to scientists like Galileo. That's not science. That's ignorance and close-mindedness masquerading as science."

Everyone went silent as Katie looked around the party. Her eyes began to well up, and she pushed Emily out of the way before running up the stairs and slamming her bedroom door shut. Emily felt terrible and stepped toward the stairs when a hand caught her shoulder.

It was Tommy and Katie's mom. "Just let her be, Emily."

"I didn't mean to—"

"It's alright. You were defending your brother, and she needs to learn she can't treat people like that." She pushed the cake in front of Tommy as they all started to sing "Happy Birthday."

What Happened?

Katie's intentions were good, but she based her alarmist prediction on evidence that wasn't entirely true. Declinism can often be fueled by our memories or by the media and popular opinion. Even if human-made global warming is a serious threat, it's doubtful that the nightmare scenario Katie envisioned will happen.

Declinism can also play a significant role in complex issues like climate change because we frequently correlate trends based on our limited observations (e.g., a specific point in time). While there is a good possibility that humans' increased carbon emissions may play a role in global warming, using unsupported evidence doesn't help the case for it.

Tuttle Twins Takeaway

Declinism happens when we see the past as better than the present and predict the future to be worse as a result. This can sometimes lead to a self-fulfilling prophecy, which can be dangerous, but it can also lead to an overreaction, which is just as bad. In overreacting, we may stoke panic and create an even worse situation than we tried to avoid.

How do we guard against this? We should use data and measurable statistics to find the truth and not rely on our memory alone. Our memory is not always a good predictor of the future. By getting an accurate understanding of where we've been and where we are now (keeping the negativity bias in mind), we can estimate a rational prediction of the future.

FRAMING EFFECT

You might think that you are forming your views independently, but the truth is that you are heavily influenced by how events and facts are framed by others.

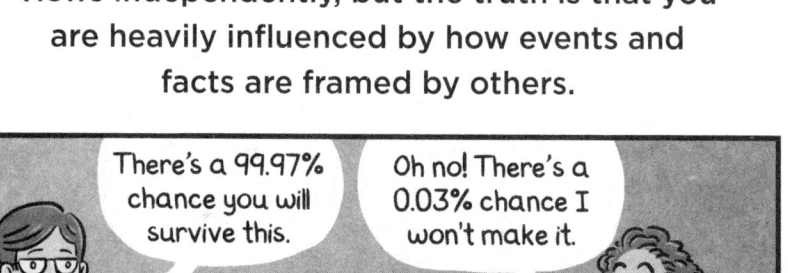

Half-Full or Half-Empty?

How we perceive something is heavily influenced by how it is framed. If a question is framed positively, chances are we'll support it (or seek risk). If a question is framed negatively, chances are we'll oppose it (or avoid risk).

Politicians, political groups, the media, and poll takers all realize this. It's one of the reasons why polls can be so far off base. Poll takers can positively frame issues they support and negatively frame issues they don't, influencing the results. News anchors employ similar tactics. A left-leaning channel may portray a story about a politician negatively. In contrast, a right-leaning channel may show that same story about that same politician positively. It's all in the framing.

You may think you're impervious to manipulation, but context and delivery alter your perception all the time. Is there anything you own that you're particularly proud of? Maybe you own a certain computer, pair of shoes, bike, piece of technology, or item of clothing that you see as a status symbol? Why are you proud of it? Is it because of the brand? What about the brand makes you proud? Is it because you perceive it's a better brand than others? Guess what. You came to that conclusion because of the context and delivery of the marketing.

Not only does the framing effect manipulate you, but you sometimes use it to push others to consider options you want them to choose. For instance, you may ask your parents if you can hang out at a friend's house, without mentioning that the friend's parents are out of town. Or you might ask if you can watch a historical movie, but fail to mention that it is violent and has explicit content.

While some studies show that the framing effect increases with age, it can uniquely affect kids and teenagers. That's because when you're younger, you tend to think in terms of whether-or-not. What does this mean? It means you're prone to considering only one choice. Should I sign up for the team or not? Should I hang out with my friend or not? Should I study for the test or not? Thinking this way increases the power of the framing effect.

If you want to reduce poor choices, it's usually good to consider three to five options. Instead of saying, should I study for the test or not? Ask yourself, should I not study at all, study for a half-hour alone, have mom or dad quiz me for a half-hour, or study with a friend for an hour? This makes it much more likely that you won't make a bad choice (not study). It's also beneficial, because listing options helps you focus on a plan.

But why does the framing effect happen? Because it saves us mental energy. When you're at a restaurant, you might tell yourself you feel like chicken or a burger and quickly narrow down your options. Could you imagine how long it would take if you considered the pros and cons of every menu item? For the little things, framing is helpful, but for the bigger things (social issues, politics, and moral questions), we must be careful it doesn't unduly influence our opinions.

The framing effect can be illustrated this way:

- Person A frames information with a positive or negative bias.

- Person B's perception is affected by Person A's positive or negative framing of the information.

An Example with Ethan and Emily

Emily and Ethan were in the middle of walking home from the park. They watched the golden leaves fall from the trees and jumped back in surprise as a wide-eyed figure lunged at them from around the corner. Ethan got in front of Emily before they realized it was their friend Pat.

"Hey!" Pat said. "How are you guys?"

Ethan moved back to Emily's side. "We're doing good. Are you alright, Pat?"

Pat held an energy drink that had Loch Ness Punch emblazoned across it. Underneath the words was a yellow dinosaur with sunglasses. As he took a sip, his hand shook. "I'm doing great, feeling great, the world is my oyster, and it's a beautiful day. A beautiful day." He grinned wide as his hand continued to shake, and some of the drink spilled out of the container.

"Are you sure you're okay?" Emily asked.

"Oh yeah, I'm doing great. Feeling great." He raised the drink and took another gulp.

"Just out of curiosity, how many of those have you had?" Ethan asked.

Pat shrugged his shoulders. "Not sure. Why?"

"You're acting... strange," Emily said.

"You mean better? Smarter? More confident? Do I look confident? I feel confident."

"Is that why you're drinking so many of those?" Ethan asked.

"It's mind juice. These things make you smarter, faster, and confident. I was a zero before I started drinking these things. Now it's like I'm flying. Everything's different."

"That's probably because of the large amounts of caffeine you're consuming," Emily said. "When was the last time you slept?"

Pat laughed at her. "That's the great thing about these. I barely need to sleep. I've got so many ideas going through my head. I never realized I could perform at this level. They help you think faster, be more productive, and get more done. Did I say that already? I bet if you and Ethan started drinking these, you'd be like superheroes, considering how smart you are already." Pat lifted the drink to his lips again as his hand shook and it spilled on his shirt.

"Um, okay," Ethan said. "But not sleeping and being this hopped up on caffeine is not good for you. Whatever benefits you're getting from drinking these are probably not worth the side effects."

Pat stared glassy-eyed right through Ethan. Ethan waved his hand in front of his face, and Pat jumped back.

"Sorry, that was a micro nap. They seem to come on inadvertently. Just a small side effect." He danced in place as he squeezed his legs together. "Well, sorry to cut this short, but I have to use the bathroom." He raised the drink in the air. "You Tuttle twins really should try it. You'll thank me later."

As Pat speed walked in the opposite direction, Emily and Ethan looked at each other, confused about why their friend started drinking the energy drinks.

What Happened?

Pat allowed the Loch Ness Punch commercial's framing to influence his judgment. He decided to drink it based only on the implied benefits and took no consideration of the costs. The commercials showed confident young people having fun together. Pat concluded that he would be like the actors—confident, fast, strong, smart—if he drank it.

The commercial made no mention of the many side effects of drinking large amounts of caffeine either (e.g., insomnia, digestive issues, increased urination, addiction, fatigue, increased heart rate). Pat was so excited about the benefits that he didn't even consider whether drinking the punch would introduce anything negative to his life.

Tuttle Twins Takeaway

Framing can have a significant impact on our decisions—not only on an individual level but also on a global level. The way the media presents information and how poll takers frame questions can alter public opinion, governmental policies, elections, and judicial decisions with far-reaching consequences.

It's great to be aware of these consequences. But how do we guard against the framing effect? Well, there are a few things you can do. First, you need to accept that you're susceptible to the framing effect and can be manipulated. Those who believe they're invulnerable are often the easiest to deceive. In realizing that you're vulnerable to being deceived by the framing effect, each time you hear new information, ask youself this question: "How is this being framed?" Is it positive or negative? Then try to reframe the information in another way.

When making decisions, it's also great to consider multiple options to limit the framing effect's power. With all of that in mind, create a lifestyle of seeking to be well-informed. People who actively seeking to learn, be involved, and get informed are usually less susceptible to the framing effect. They're more likely to see past the manipulation and make better decisions.

ATTRIBUTION ERROR

When you mess up, you're likely to excuse your error due to any number of explainable circumstances. But when others mess up, you're likely to assume it's a reflection of their poor character.

They Have Issues

The attribution error means that we're willing to cut ourselves slack far more than we are for others. Suppose you come across someone yelling at a teary-eyed waitress. You might assume that they're a jerk until you realize they caught her stealing another waitress's tip. If you see a stranger in dirty clothes, you might assume they're a slob and never consider they had to crawl underneath their neighbor's porch to rescue a stray cat. Or maybe you see someone singing "Twinkle Twinkle Little Star" in the grocery store. You might think they're certifiably insane and never realize it helps calm down their socially anxious child, who is hiding behind their leg.

These behaviors all had a good reason, but it was easier to assume that they were a result of their character and not external circumstances. Now think about yourself. Have you ever lost your temper, arrived late, or spilled something on your clothes? Did you blame your poor character? Or did you cut yourself some slack based on the situation? You likely attributed this behavior to the circumstances and not your personality, unless poor behavior or lateness is a repeated pattern in your life. But strangers who saw you might have assumed that you are naturally ill-tempered, disrespectful, and sloppy. How could they judge you based on one isolated incident? That's not fair! Well, for the same reason that you judged those other people.

The attribution error doesn't have to be negative all the time. It can be positive too. For instance, you may find that you like a particular actor or actress. You think they're great, and while they may be excellent at acting, the attribution error makes you believe they are a good person. The character they portray might be nothing like who they are in real life. Yet, we unconsciously assume that they're behaving this way because of their personality.

The attribution error is how our brain makes judgments from limited information. Sometimes, this can be unfair, as we don't consider what led to someone's behavior. We only assume that their behavior is a reflection of who they are. At other times, it may be close to the truth, but we should still realize it's not fair to label someone negatively. There likely could be a good reason for their behavior. This doesn't excuse bad behavior, but it helps us understand each other better and give others some grace in the same measure that we hope they would give us on our bad days.

The attribution error is composed of:

- Person A sees Person B exhibit a behavior.

- Person A automatically assumes this is typical behavior for Person B and attributes it to their nature.

An Example with Ethan and Emily

Emily and Ethan were enjoying the last days of summer. The air was beginning to cool, it was a little windy, and they could feel it wouldn't be long before the leaves started to change. Emily rode her scooter as Ethan rolled alongside her on a skateboard. They passed their friend George's house, and as they did, they saw him in his window, peering out of it with binoculars. Emily waved at him as George slowly waved back and dipped below the windowsill.

"Let's go see if he wants to hang out," Ethan said.

They rolled down his driveway, and George looked around as if someone might be watching.

"What are you doing? Birdwatching?" Emily asked.

George grunted. "I'm trying to catch the bike thief. Some kid stole my bike. I'm not sure who, but my mom called me in for lunch, and when I went back outside to get my bike, it was gone."

"That's terrible," Ethan said. "If you want, you can borrow my bike."

George grunted again. "Thanks, but I loved that bike. I would…" George's jaw dropped in surprise.

Emily and Ethan turned as they watched a much younger boy riding the same bike that George owned. It was black with orange tires and neon green lights in the spokes. While this one had training wheels attached, the odds of someone else having an identical bike were tiny. Before Emily and Ethan realized it, George jumped out of the window, stomped through his mom's peony bushes, and chased after the boy like an angry dog. The boy looked back, surprised, and pedaled faster down the sidewalk.

"Stop, thief! Stop! Police!"

The boy picked up speed as his training wheels rattled, and Emily and Ethan jumped on their scooter and skateboard, heading down the street after the two of them. Despite the other kid being on a bike, George gained on him and tackled the kid into their neighbor's lawn. Emily and Ethan came upon the scene as the kid wailed and George wrestled the bike away from him.

"You're going away for a long, long time," George said. "We caught you red-handed."

The boy continued groaning on the ground. His one leg had been badly scraped up and was starting to swell.

"What are you talking about?"

"You stole my bike. You're a criminal."

The kid looked up at George, confused. He was young, maybe about six years old. "I didn't steal your bike. It was in the garbage." He whimpered and clutched his leg.

"No, you stole it. It wasn't in the garbage."

The boy looked at Emily and Ethan. "It was. It was right next to the garbage can at the curb. I thought you were throwing it out. I wouldn't have taken it if I didn't think it was garbage."

Emily bent down and touched the kid's leg. It was getting more and more swollen, and he cried as she felt it. She stood up and folded her arms. "It's broken, George. You broke this kid's leg."

"Well, I didn't mean to, but he deserved it."

"Did you leave it by the trash can on garbage day?" Ethan asked gruffly.

George shrugged his shoulders. "Maybe. I can't remember. Don't tell me you're taking his side now?"

Ethan looked at Emily. "You stay with him. I'll go see if I can call an ambulance from Ms. Jones's house."

As Ethan ran next door, Emily comforted the boy by the side of the road.

What Happened?

George assumed a thief stole his bike and that the boy riding his bike was that thief. In doing this, he committed the attribution error. Instead of giving the boy the benefit of the doubt, George assumed that it was his character to steal bikes. If he asked himself if there could be another reason, he might have understood that leaving the bike next to the garbage created confusion.

Had George considered that whoever was riding his bike might not be a thief, he wouldn't have approached the situation so forcefully. He wouldn't have run at the boy screaming, tackled him, and broken his leg. George had been so sure that he was in the right, that this boy was a criminal, and that tackling him was justified. In the end, it was George's actions—not the boy's—that were wrong.

Tuttle Twins Takeaway

It's almost instinctual to attribute others' behaviors to their character. When you catch yourself doing this, try to give others the benefit of the doubt. Remember those times when you might have behaved similarly due to an unusual circumstance. Until you're able to find out more, be willing to show grace and cut them some slack. Don't assume that what you believe is correct.

One of the best ways to overcome this bias is by getting to know someone better. Take the time to listen, find out more, and even let them vent. You might find that your initial instinct was wrong. In those instances when you don't have the time for this—for example, strangers you likely will never see again—it doesn't hurt to assume the best and move on.

Finally, when you find yourself behaving poorly, instead of justifying and blaming, try to take personal responsibility for your actions. While everyone makes mistakes and might have good excuses, we need to understand that doesn't mean bad behavior is acceptable. By taking responsibility for our failures, we become conscious of them and make them less likely to occur in the future.

Elect
Bob Smith
ACTUAL SOLUTIONS
TO THE BIGGEST PROBLEMS
CHAZ
SNAZOLLA
WE CAN DO THIS!
Chaz Snazolla definitely looks more presidential.

HALO EFFECT

Our judgments about another person are often influenced by how much we like them or how attractive they are. Beware, because appearances can be deceiving!

Perfect in Every Way

Relationships are important. Our lives revolve around relationships. As we grow, we decide whom to be friends with, whom to work with, and whom to marry. We have to make judgments as to who the best people are to fill these roles. The people we associate with can either lift us up or bring us down. Our future can depend on choosing the right people.

But before we can choose the right people, we must understand what qualities are important and find the people who best exhibit those qualities. Honesty, integrity, loyalty, and reliability are all great qualities to look for in others. Except sometimes, instead of choosing people who exhibit the best qualities, we choose people based on unrelated attributes.

We might choose someone good-looking, funny, or charming to be friends with and not realize that they have none of the other qualities we're looking for in a friend. Even worse, they might have several negative attributes that we didn't consider. Simultaneously, we might miss out on a great friendship with someone who has all of the right qualities but isn't as attractive, funny, or charming as the person we chose.

Unfortunately, the halo effect is an unfair bias that's all around us. As mentioned, it affects friendships, but it can also influence interviews, promotions, elections, courtroom decisions, tips for waiters, and even grades. The halo effect can cause us to make faulty judgments based on more than just looks. We can fixate on any quality that people find attractive. It could be enthusiasm, humor, or confidence. In focusing on the desirable quality, we find ourselves assuming their other attributes will be equivalent.

The halo effect has a significant impact on our relationships, but did you know it can also apply to brands and products? Sometimes, buzzwords on products can even engender the halo effect. Words like fat-free or organic might sway someone to buy a product that isn't remarkably different than the competitor, except for the inclusion of the words on the container.

Like the attribution error, the halo effect results from a quick judgment of someone based on limited information. We see the attractive quality and assume this person's other attributes will be at the same level. There's nothing wrong with believing the best, but it's unfair when it causes us to play favorites. Someone could be a strong candidate for something, yet we may choose the less qualified person because we consider them more likable or attractive. When we judge based on the halo effect, it can hurt us, too, as we discover the person we favored is less than expected. In time, this can put a strain on both ends of the relationship and create resentments and conflict.

The halo effect happens when:

- Person A considers several people based on specific criteria.

- Person B exhibits an appealing yet unrelated quality.

- Person A assumes Person B's other character traits are favorable and gives them preference.

An Example with Ethan and Emily

Emily and Ethan strolled through their summer camp's cafeteria and sat down with their lunch at their almost-empty table. Usually, they sat with eight or nine of their friends, but today it was only them and Audrey. Across the cafeteria, several kids huddled around one table. There wasn't a square inch of open sitting space. Ethan noticed several of his friends, who usually sat at their table, squeezed in among them.

"What's going on?" Ethan asked.

"There's a new kid," Audrey said.

Ethan shrugged his shoulders. "There are new kids all the time. What's so special about this one?"

Emily took a bite of her sandwich and looked at her brother. "You didn't hear? It's Calvin from Calvin's World."

Ethan cocked his head. "Calvin's what?"

"Calvin's World," Audrey said. "It's only the biggest show on YouTube right now. He's famous."

Ethan shrugged his shoulders again. "Okay, good for him."

Suddenly, a short, blonde-haired kid stood up, and many of the kids around the table followed him across the cafeteria. Ethan could only assume it was Calvin. As the boy approached the garbage can, he tossed his plastic tray at it from several feet away. The tray bounced off the rim, and food went everywhere, some of it spraying against Ethan's back.

Calvin laughed. "You just got Calvined!" He pointed, stuck out his tongue, and made a fist with his pinky and thumb out as he waved it in Ethan's face.

Ethan glared at him, and Calvin moved on, but not before several of his followers had a chance to make the same silly sign in Ethan's face. As they imitated their hero, Calvin grabbed a piece of pizza out of another kid's hand, took a bite, and dropped it back in the kid's lap as several people laughed. The kid looked down at his stained lap, annoyed.

Emily wiped the back of Ethan's shirt. "He doesn't seem very nice."

"That's an understatement," Ethan said.

What Happened?

Many of the kids in the cafeteria, including Ethan and Emily's friends, allowed the halo effect to influence their judgment of Calvin. He was rude, messy, lazy, and inconsiderate of others. Usually, when deciding on a friend, these characteristics would be enough to make the decision obvious. However, many of the kids saw Calvin's minor celebrity status as an attractive quality.

This was enough for them to excuse or overlook his other negative traits. The sad thing is that the halo effect can be a lose-lose-lose scenario. Ethan's friends lose because they choose a lousy friend over a good one. Ethan loses because his friends decide to focus on Calvin over him. But the one who loses the most is Calvin. Sometimes, if the halo is strong enough, the person with the halo may get by without addressing their negative qualities. This can end up stunting their personal growth and their maturity. As their halo fades over time, others will outgrow them, and they can be left behind.

Tuttle Twins Takeaway

We know the halo effect happens when we come across someone with an attractive attribute and assume this extends to their other character traits. For instance, because they're funny, they must also be friendly. If they aren't, we may overlook it as we try to rectify reality with the illusion in our heads. Not only does this bias affect our judgment, but when we give unearned preferential treatment, it's unfair to others.

How do we counteract it? Take your time and slow down your thought process. If you can, make a list of essential attributes and focus on those. Set the attractive quality aside and ask yourself if you'd still rate the person as a good friend/candidate/leader based on their other characteristics. Would they still be at the top of your list? Be honest.

Give yourself time to really consider this and time to view all of your potential choices in this new light. Lastly, while beauty, humor, or many other attributes might seem rare, remember there are billions of people in the world. Their attractive characteristics may seem unique but are likely shared by millions across the globe.

OPTIMISM BIAS

People can have a tendency to overestimate the likelihood of a positive outcome. This wishful thinking may seem nice but doesn't help us make an informed decision.

I've never had any serious medical issues. I'm as fit as a fiddle.

I'll never need an insurance policy like this.

Every other hot dog stand in this location failed, but mine won't!

My vegan, gluten-free dogs will make all the difference.

We can totally do this job by ourselves. My schedule is open.

How long could renovating a kitchen take —a weekend?

It Will Be Fine

We're wired to be positive. Believing good things will come can improve our mood, health, happiness, and self-perception. Optimism is generally seen as a pretty good thing. When we are optimistic, it can also lead to a self-fulfilling prophecy. In believing that we'll be successful, we're more likely to act in ways that will make us successful. Optimism motivates us to reach the goals that we set. If we weren't optimistic about those goals and didn't think that they were achievable, it would make achieving them even more difficult. We would feel we were wasting our time.

As the adage goes, though, sometimes even optimism can be "too much of a good thing." Someone under the optimism bias makes poor decisions because they feel that nothing terrible will happen. This tends to happen more when we feel like we're in control. This bias can take two forms: positive (we overestimate our chance of success) or negative (we underestimate the likelihood of failure). Yet, they're flip sides of the same coin.

You may overestimate how well you'll do on a test while underestimating its difficulty and the length of time it will take to study. You might overestimate how quickly you can complete a new task and underestimate the obstacles that might arise or how long it will take to learn a new skill. You could overestimate the odds of winning a basketball game while underestimating the amount of effort and practice it will take. As a result, you might find yourself performing poorly and getting benched—unsure of what happened.

We also routinely rely on this bias when an event is unlikely or infrequent. We tell ourselves that everything will be alright and nothing bad will happen, so we don't need to worry or take any precautions. This can save us from worrying about unlikely events or expending mental energy on them. But it can also lead to risky behaviors that endanger lives. Someone might not wear a seat belt or a helmet because they think the likelihood of getting into an accident is small. Someone else may not evacuate their home when a hurricane warning is issued because they believe the hurricane won't be that bad. Another person may forgo routine medical evaluations because the risk of discovering a health problem may be low.

While the optimism bias can affect individuals, it can also play a larger role in financial markets, politics, government policies, and business decisions. Businesses and politicians can believe nothing awful will happen and fail to prepare for changes to the market or global economy. At one time, people could not have imagined that companies like Kodak, Blockbuster, and Toys R Us could possibly fail. Likewise, some people refused to acknowledge the coming of the 2008 financial crisis even as it loomed on the horizon. Optimism bias prevented them from seeing reality and acting appropriately.

Researchers have studied ways to eliminate the optimism bias in medicine. They've discovered that in trying to educate people and counteract the natural tendency to assume bad health problems won't happen to an individual, they were accidentally invoking the backfire effect (causing people to be even more optimistic). This finding might lead us to wonder if there is any hope against the optimism bias.

The optimism bias happens as follows:

- Person A fails to consider adverse outcomes.

- Person A assumes everything will be fine and nothing bad will happen, regardless of the likelihood.

An Example with Ethan and Emily

Emily and Ethan licked their ice cream as they stood outside the pet store watching several black and brown Labrador puppies wrestle with each other. They laughed as one puppy bit his sibling too hard and both went tumbling over.

"They're so cute," Emily said.

"Maybe someday," Ethan said. "Puppies are a lot of responsibility."

"I know, but they're so cute," Emily squealed.

Emily felt a hand on her shoulder and turned to see her friend Lisa. "Hi, Emily. Are you getting a puppy, too?"

Emily shook her head and frowned. "Unfortunately, no. Puppies are a lot of work, and I don't have the time right now."

"My mom and dad finally said I could get one, if I can prove I would be a good pet owner," Lisa said, ignoring Emily's comment.

"They did?" Ethan asked while trying not to sound surprised.

Thinking about Lisa's room, it wasn't exactly the best environment for a dog. Emily had told him stories of how it was so messy that she didn't even know what color the carpet was. A permanent layer of clothes, toys, and food wrappers covered it. From his understanding, Lisa wasn't exactly the most responsible kid in the world either. She had adopted and accidentally killed more goldfish than anyone he knew!

"It's going to be great. I'm going to sleep with it, snuggle with it, and love it to death."

"I hope you love the smell of puppy pee in the morning," Ethan joked.

Lisa gave him a funny look. "What?"

"You know you'll have to house-train them, right?" Emily said.

Lisa wrinkled up her nose. "I thought they came pre-house-trained. Don't they have those options?"

"They're not cars," Ethan said.

Lisa shrugged her shoulders, "Well, I guess my parents could do that when they get home from work in the evenings."

"They said you had to prove you would be a good pet owner, right?" Emily asked, confused.

"Yeah, but I thought that meant picking out cute outfits and figuring out which collar and food dish would make the best accessories."

"You shouldn't be getting a dog if you're not prepared to take care of it," Ethan said.

Lisa waved him off. "Don't worry about it. I'm sure it will all work out. What's the worst that can happen? "

"The poor animal might suffer," Emily said.

"Stop being such a downer." Lisa tapped on the glass and grinned as the puppies in the window yelped at her. "You're overthinking this. It'll be fine." She pushed her way into the store and scooped up one of the puppies.

What Happened?

Getting a puppy is exciting. Lisa couldn't wait to get one, but she was blind to possible adverse outcomes. She didn't think about all the hard work involved or how she would even prove to her parents that she was responsible enough to take care of one. She was so busy dreaming about how much fun she would have snuggling with her puppy that she didn't think about all the things she would need to do to be a responsible pet owner.

Sometimes, the optimism bias can lead us to make bad decisions. Usually, these decisions affect only us. But when those decisions concern other people or animals, our optimism bias can also unintentionally end up hurting them, too.

Tuttle Twins Takeaway

Optimism can be beneficial. We need optimism so that we can accomplish our goals. A world without optimism would be a bleak and sad place. We also naturally tend to be optimistic, but it can be dangerous when we don't look realistically at the situation. When we don't assess the likelihood of adverse outcomes and instead overestimate the positives, we can put ourselves and others in a difficult position.

We can improve our ability to see and avoid optimism bias. First, we can separate ourselves from the situation. Think about what would be the likelihood of someone else having a positive outcome if they stepped into our shoes. In taking our egos out of the equation, we can look more objectively at possible consequences.

The second thing we can do is imagine it's the future, and the outcome wasn't positive but negative. In this imaginary scenario, ask what might have gone wrong and why. This can also help you consider potential adversity and overcome the blindness of the optimism bias.

And finally, if time plays a role, then use time management. Implementing a deadline with a plan that details how long it will take to do each step will give you a better chance of realistically accomplishing your goals.

PESSIMISM BIAS

People can have a tendency to overestimate the likelihood of a negative outcome. This defense mechanism against potential disappointment can limit your opportunity for positive outcomes.

It's Not Worth It

Pessimism and the negativity bias seem very similar on the surface. The simple fact is the negativity bias means we believe there is more bad in the world than good. In contrast, the pessimism bias is a belief that nothing will turn out well, no matter the situation. This might mean you believe you will fail a test, even though you studied hard and did quite well on past tests. Another person might think their interview will go badly, even though they have all the necessary experience and qualifications for the position. Still another person might never talk to a potential friend because they're afraid of rejection. The thing is, when you're under the influence of the pessimism bias, it can permeate every aspect of your life, causing all of these attitudes at different times.

Even when something good happens, the pessimism bias can make you think that something terrible is just around the corner. Pessimists can believe that life is a painful struggle. Sometimes, we might adopt this bias because we're afraid of getting our hopes up. It feels safer and less scary to be prepared for the worst than it does to be disappointed. Most of the time, the worst never happens, but sometimes, this can become another self-fulfilling prophecy. This is especially true in situations where confidence plays a role, like interviewing, public speaking, or going on a date. We expect the worst, prepare for the worst, and, in so doing, make it happen. This only strengthens the belief that nothing good will come our way.

While the optimism bias and pessimism bias seem like polar opposites, the funny thing is that they can have the same result. With the optimism bias, we don't prepare because we believe success is guaranteed, and with the pessimism bias, we don't prepare because we believe success is impossible. In both tendencies, we're left unprepared, which increases our chances of failure.

Even though both fail to prepare, optimists can have the upper hand as they're more likely to press forward, while the pessimist is more apt to quit. Pessimists tend to give up more easily. This tendency to always expect failure can cause them to lean toward depression, which is one of pessimism's most noticeable side effects. If ignored, a pessimistic attitude can become dangerous to our mental health, as depression, anxiety, and other problems arise.

Even though pessimism can be a problem, it can also provide motivation. The difference between it being a demotivating factor or a motivating factor depends on whether it's negative or positive. Negative pessimism assumes you'll fail and should give up. However, positive pessimism admits there's a difficult challenge, but success is still possible. This type of pessimism can help you better prepare, improve your coping skills, and counter the optimism bias. It can also be helpful in dangerous (e.g., life-threatening) situations or when failure is absolute.

The pessimism bias includes:

- Person A considers possible outcomes of a situation.

- Person A assumes everything will go wrong and nothing good will happen, regardless of the likelihood.

An Example with Ethan and Emily

Ethan and Emily walked down the line and slapped hands with the other kickball team. It was evident from the smiles on Emily and Ethan's team's faces and the frowns on the other team's faces who had won.

"I can't believe that we made it this far," Ethan said, as he and Emily slapped the last of the other team's hands and then high-fived each other. "We made it to the playoffs. Who would've thought?"

"We're going to have to focus," Emily said. "We can't let up. We can't take anything for granted. The other team is really good."

"Too good," their teammate Walter said as he walked up to them with a frown on his face. "There's no way we can ever beat them. They've won the championship five years in a row."

"Yes, but a lot of their older players aged out last year. We have a good chance of beating them if we work hard and don't get cocky," Ethan said.

"Who are you kidding? We don't have a shot, and it's going to be embarrassing. We'll be the laughing stock of the county. We have no business playing that game."

Emily frowned. "Walter, you act like it's impossible. It's not like we're talking about winning the gold medal in the Olympics. We're just saying that if we focus and work together as a team, there's a possibility we can win the local youth kickball championships. Why are you so adamant that we won't?"

Walter rolled his neck. "When we get crushed, you'll see I'm right."

He walked away, and Ethan wiped the sweat from his forehead. "Not exactly a great pep talk before the big championship, is it?"

"Why do I suddenly feel like we have no chance?" Emily asked as the rest of their team poured Gatorade over their coach.

What Happened?

Pessimism can be positive if it helps us prepare for the challenges in our lives. But it can be negative when it convinces us to give up. Emily's and Ethan's was the former but Walter's pessimism was the latter. He refused to believe they had any possible chance of winning and was adamant that it was hopeless. He also overestimated the severity of shame that would come from losing. It's unlikely people would laugh at them no matter the outcome of the game.

The other thing about both positive and negative pessimism is that they can be contagious. Ethan and Emily weren't overly optimistic. They knew success wasn't going to be simple and conceded that, yet Walter put strong doubts in their heads. His position was so extreme that it made them wonder if they were overly optimistic about having any chance of winning the kickball championships. If his pessimism spreads throughout the team, there is a good chance that losing will become a self-fulfilling prophecy. The same can be true for positive pessimism. Walter could have chosen to find hope from Emily's and Ethan's words of encouragement but unfortunately he didn't. Emily and Ethan can't control how their other teammates will respond to their encouragement but their team will benefit if they can continue to offer it.

Tuttle Twins Takeaway

The pessimism bias can affect every area of our lives and encourage doubts that become self-fulfilling prophecies—we're never successful if we never try. Even worse, it can be harmful to our mental health. Worry, anxiety, and depression are common side effects of pessimism. If not dealt with, it can lead to mental health problems.

If you're affected by the pessimism bias, a good thing you can do is slow down your decision-making process. Don't rush to conclusions. Instead of saying success is impossible, realize instead that it will be difficult. Take the time to consider the different outcomes, the problems that could cause each one, and the solutions to those problems. For instance, you might apply this line of questioning: How could it fail? Why? What can I do about it? Use the answers to these questions to help you develop a plan of attack. This is called positive pessimism, and it can help you prepare and press forward rather than give up at the first sign of difficulty.

Lastly, an excellent way to increase your confidence is to visualize past successes in a similar area of your life. This will help you to see the problem more objectively and understand that you have succeeded before and can succeed again.

JUST-WORLD HYPOTHESIS

Many people tend to think that evil is always punished and that good is always rewarded, but the reality of our situation is often much more nuanced than this.

Finally, karma is punishing her for what she did to me those many years ago.

It's the poetic pendulum of justice.

Well, Tommy had it coming.

A guy like him shouldn't have been hanging around in that neighborhood late at night.

Turns out he's extremely wealthy.

He must have worked very hard to deserve that kind of lifestyle.

It's Karma, Baby

We want to believe that the world is just. That when we work hard or do good there will be some tacit reward, or that when a crime is committed there will be some form of punishment. This belief can help us to be less fearful and more optimistic. It gives us a sense of control and meaning, but it's a coping mechanism.

Every injustice isn't always punished, and every good deed isn't always rewarded. For instance, someone could smoke for their entire life and not get lung cancer, while someone else who never smoked could. A violent criminal may win the lottery, while someone who worked hard their entire life may end up losing their job and retirement money in an economic downturn.

The just-world hypothesis grows out of our inability to accept this reality. Instead of conceding life is unfair, we assume it's fair. Have you ever heard the idioms, "What goes around comes around," "Their chickens have come home to roost," or "They got what was coming to them"? All of these are based on the just-world hypothesis.

Through it, we conclude successful people are more fortunate because they're more deserving. We reason that everything they have is a result of their hard work and intelligence. They earned everything they have. We don't consider that their success could have resulted from luck or unethical behavior, even though both are possible.

But the big problem with assuming there is justice is that we rationalize injustice. We can end up believing that someone else's suffering is warranted. Instead of empathizing and feeling bad, we conclude that they brought it upon themselves. In blaming others for their suffering, we have an excuse to be detached. We don't feel the need to be compassionate or do anything to help alleviate their pain.

In the Bible, the book of Job is an excellent example of this. Job suffers a series of seemingly unrelated calamities. He loses his kids, wealth, and health. You would think his friends would try and console him, but, instead, they blame him for everything that occurs. They assume that he must have done something wrong for all this to happen. This might seem irrational, but just like Job's friends, we can do the same thing. Even when there is no correlation between someone's actions and their suffering, we can wonder if there is some unseen force behind it all. Is God punishing them?

Don't misunderstand; Someone's worldview has nothing to do with this bias. Although a religious person may call it God, others may call it karma, the universe, or something else entirely. It affects all of us. When we see senseless suffering, we try to protect our innate desire for order in the world by rationalizing a reason for the suffering.

The first step in overcoming the just-world hypothesis is realizing that injustice exists. While we all have some control over our lives, many things are beyond our control. A person's status as a world leader or an inmate on death row doesn't necessarily mean they are deserving of their situation. Sometimes, bad people are rewarded; sometimes good people suffer. Try to have empathy and compassion before placing blame.

The just-world hypothesis takes place when:

- Person A blames Person B for their own suffering, and/or Person A admires Person C for their success.
- Person A decides that each outcome was the result of each one's behavior.

An Example with Ethan and Emily

Ethan and Emily walked out of church and breathed in the fresh air. Many people smiled and greeted each other as they exited the building. They stood at the side of the building, waiting for their parents to come out. The Tuttle twins were used to waiting a while after church because their father had a habit of talking to a lot of people along the way.

Ethan looked at his watch. He was in no rush to be anywhere, but it was a lovely day, and he wanted to enjoy it. Emily touched his shoulder and pointed to a boy who had tears in his eyes as a woman spoke to him. Ethan almost didn't recognize him. It was their class bully, Simon. The woman wiped his tears and pulled him closer as he sobbed on her shoulder. For as long as Ethan could remember, Simon had always been a bully. When he was smaller, he used to push Ethan down on the playground and call him names. Ethan had stepped up and put a stop to it a long time ago, but Simon had never stopped being a bully. He still picked on other kids and always tried to be the tough guy. Ethan couldn't remember a time he had ever seen him flinch, let alone cry.

"Hey, guys." Raj walked up to them and stood by Emily's side as they all tried to hide the fact that they were watching Simon cry. "Can you believe it?"

Emily smacked her lips. "What happened?"

"His grandmother died. I guess they were close."

Ethan and Emily couldn't help feeling bad for Simon. Even though he is a bully, it was sad to see him suffering.

Raj smirked. "It's sad, but he got what he deserves."

"What?" Ethan asked.

"If he weren't such a bully, maybe she would still be alive."

"Are you saying that his grandma died because he's a bully?" Emily asked.

Raj shrugged his shoulders. "You reap what you sow."

Ethan turned toward him. "First of all, those two things aren't connected. Do you think God killed his grandmother because he took your lunch money when we were in the first grade?"

Raj raised his eyebrows and held them there. "God works in mysterious ways. Who am I to say what He is or isn't doing?"

Simon walked over to them and blinked slowly at Ethan.

"Sorry for your loss," whispered Ethan.

"Yeah, sorry for your loss, Simon," Emily said.

Simon started to blubber and pushed his face into Ethan's shoulder as he cried. Raj turned to them and mouthed the words, "You reap what you sow," as Ethan patted Simon's shoulder.

What Happened?

When Raj heard Simon had lost his grandmother, he felt terrible for him, but then he remembered all the bad things he had done. This allowed Raj to conclude that Simon had brought this on himself. Detaching himself from the situation meant he didn't have to empathize, and he could even revel in it.

He truly believed Simon was getting what he deserved without ever asking if it was fair or logical. While Raj's bias was religion based, the just-world hypothesis doesn't require a god. One could also believe in a supernatural force, the universe, or some karmic law. Even a devout atheist may laugh at a situation while speaking about it, but all the while wonder what happened.

Tuttle Twins Takeaway

We all have moments throughout our lives where luck rewards us through no cause of our own. Likewise, we all suffer and experience pain due to circumstances beyond our control. Just because someone is blessed or struggling, it's good to remember neither is necessarily deserved. When we blame and point fingers, we devalue others. Before we jump to conclusions, we should consider the person's environment, social pressures, cultural expectations, and all the other reasons for their situation. While these don't excuse bad behavior, they at least provide an understanding of what might be influencing it. Everyone has different experience and make mistakes. And sometimes bad things happen to good people (and vice versa).

IN-GROUP BIAS

We like to think that we are impartial, but our minds lead us to favor people who are part of our group because of our shared connection.

It's Good to Be Us

We all want to believe that we're fair with everyone, but that isn't necessarily the case. We instinctively favor those who share our characteristics or belong to groups we identify with. This might be most evident in the school lunchroom. One table may be largely cheerleaders. Another table could be kids who love role-playing games, and another table may be mostly wrestlers. Through these shared characteristics, groups form. This might not always be so straightforward, but every group consists of members who share something in common.

In-group bias can be a good thing, as you don't have the time to get to know all the kids in your school or town. It gives you a chance to whittle down your options quickly and focus your attention on people who most likely share a common interest with you. Instead of the impossible task of getting to know everyone well, you save time and energy by focusing on those most similar to you first.

You've been doing this a long time, too. Do you remember the first time you made friends? Did you favor someone just because you liked the same color or popsicle flavor? While you've come a long way since then, it's easy to see how ingrained this bias is in us. It's as if we instinctively prefer those who share some of our characteristics or beliefs.

While it may seem harmless, the sad part about this bias is that it can also cause us to be unfair. We put others into groups and don't look beyond the label we attach. In short, as we favor some, we unintentionally alienate others. Even while trying to counteract this bias, it may prove difficult. You may prefer someone who likes the same football team as you while ignoring someone who likes the rival team. What you fail to realize is that you have more in common with the person who enjoys the rival, only you never get the opportunity to learn that because of the in-group bias.

Not only does it affect friendships, but it can influence all areas of society, from a court's decisions to the way the media portrays someone. A judge may favor someone who shares their religion, or a news anchor may be more sympathetic towards someone who shares their political views. Because it's so prevalent and affects us every day, we usually don't notice this bias but it can become extreme. Throughout history, there were times when different political parties and groups have used the in-group bias to their advantage. They have used it as a tool to divide people and gain power. In the process, they stoked racism, xenophobia, anti-semitism, and bigotry that resulted in untold suffering.

Today, we find ourselves in a unique time. Critical Race Theory seems well-intentioned, as it seeks to address in-group bias related to race or racism. While it's good for us to examine ourselves and address any bias, critical race theory seeks to address it in only one race. It insinuates that this bias is distinct to that particular race (in its DNA) and is not reflective of all people. This is problematic as not only is it false, but it's also divisive. It takes something we all share, exaggerates it, and claims all members of a single group are racist while other groups are not.

Anyone who has opened a history book realizes that dividing people based on race and blaming one race for society's problems is never a great idea. And we are all vulnerable to this bias. The flawed claim that in-group bias is the domain of one specific race doesn't give us an excuse to ignore it. We still have to address it. But how?

Instead of blaming and pointing fingers at each other, perhaps the best place to start, as it is with all things, is within ourselves. Try to put yourself in the shoes of those in other groups. Look at those in your group as if you didn't share a commonality as well. Also, find opportunities to cooperate with people outside of your group. Find causes or goals you might share. The key to a better world isn't through condemnation but rather with cooperation.

The in-group bias usually has these components:

- Person A relates to Person B and C based on shared characteristics.

- Person D doesn't exhibit the shared characteristics.

- Person A favors Person B and C in some way but not Person D.

An Example with Ethan and Emily

Emily looked at the pond water under the microscope in her homeschool co-op. Her eyes widened as she watched all the microbes swimming in the liquid. "Cool! Ethan, I see an arthropod. Wait, is that a hydra?" She twisted the focal knob. "Oh my gosh, there's a dielptus. It's hunting microbes with its proboscis! You got to see this."

Emily glanced up from the microscope toward Ethan. He nodded in her direction and continued talking with Kevin about last night's football game. Didn't he care? Emily looked back into the microscope as the dileptus swam toward the edge.

She looked back up and hit Ethan's shoulder. "Ethan. You're going to miss it. It's moving toward the edge."

He nodded again as Kevin continued talking.

"Can I see?" Marcy asked.

Emily moved aside, and Marcy looked into the microscope. "That's so cool! Wow, I just saw it eat another microbe!"

Emily smiled. "I could look at this stuff all day. It would be the best job."

Marcy scratched her head. "Hey, Emily. Are you interested in joining the Future Scientists of America Club?"

"The Future Scientists of America Club? I didn't know there was a chapter here," Emily said giddily.

"Yeah. We just started it. Right now, it's just Stacy, Ben, and me. We're looking for new members."

"What kind of commitment does it involve?"

"We have weekly lunch meetings where we discuss science. That's about it for now."

Emily smiled and glanced over at Ethan. "What about Ethan and my other friends? Can they sit with us during lunch too?"

Marcy smacked her lips. "How do I say this? Ethan and your other friends aren't exactly FSA material."

Emily smiled, unsure whether Marcy was joking or not. "What do you mean? They're smart."

"Emily, this club is only for serious scientists. We can't just let anyone be a part of it."

"So, you're saying I have to choose Future Scientists of America or Ethan and my other friends?"

Marcy sighed. "Emily, wouldn't you like to have intellectual conversations for a change? Talk with others who care about science as much as you do?"

"Yeah, but do I have to only be in one group or the other?"

Marcy folded her arms and Ethan looked over at Emily.

"Ready for lunch?" he asked.

Emily looked from Ethan to Marcy as she tried to figure out what to do.

What Happened?

To Marcy, there are two groups of people in the world, those who live for science and those who don't. She believed Emily was with her in the first group. Marcy had no interest in associating with kids who didn't love science. She was building her new club of only like-minded people. There could have been several reasons Marcy did this. Maybe she didn't want to compete for Emily's friendship, or perhaps she didn't feel comfortable with people who thought differently than she did.

In the end, she tried to convince Emily that if she conceded, she would be rewarded (i.e., accepted into a select group). This could be how someone might pressure you. They might insinuate that their group members are superior to others and that you can gain this benefit through membership. They then might force you to choose between their group and another.

Tuttle Twins Takeaway

While there's nothing wrong with belonging to a group, it isn't fair for us to favor someone strictly on the basis of them belonging to our group. What's important to remember is that we all have differences and similarities. We can find something in common with almost anyone if we try.

Always look for ways to address it in yourself. Can you see from the perspective of someone in another group? Take time to imagine yourself as a part of another group and detach yourself from the groups you may belong to as you try to see objectively.

Cooperation can also lower our in-group bias. Try to find ways to cooperate with people who don't belong to some of the groups you associate with. Seeking out diversity is important, but claiming you're absolved of bias while pointing it out in others is destructive and will only create further division.

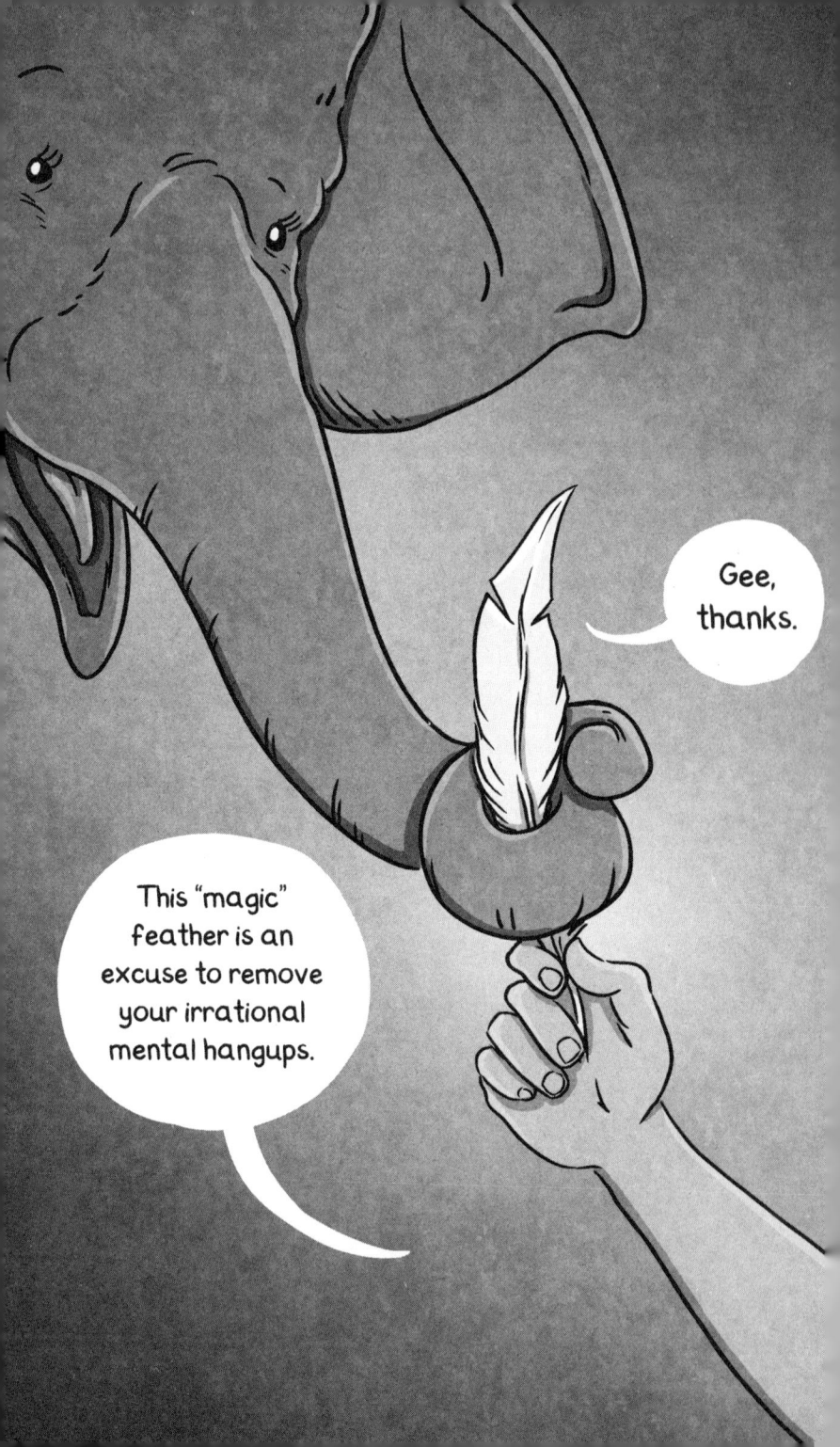

PLACEBO EFFECT

Our mind is so powerful that it can make us believe that a certain medication, practice, or circumstance has an effect us on when really it doesn't.

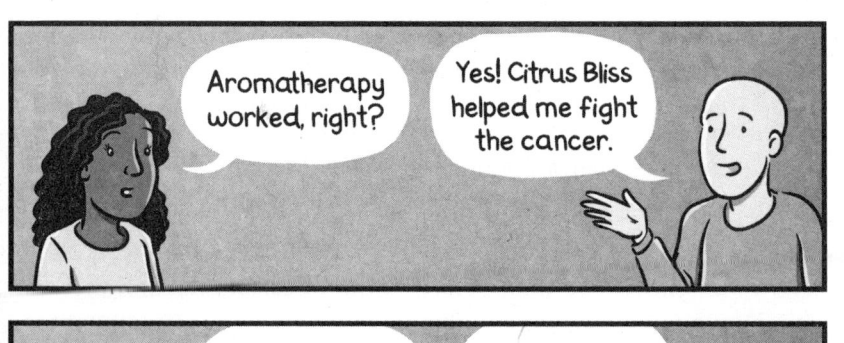

I'm Getting Better!

A placebo is typically a fake pill (e.g., sugar pill) that should not have any noticeable effects. Researchers use them to determine the effectiveness of a drug in trials. By prescribing some patients placebos and other patients the trial drug, they can find out if the drug is effective. Through this, scientists discovered some patients experience the benefits of the medication without actually taking it. In believing that the placebo will work, we fool our brain into perceiving that it does. People routinely express changes in levels of pain, depression, or fatigue after taking a placebo—in some cases, even when they know it's a placebo!

This might have to do with something called classical conditioning. The most famous case of this was Pavlov's dog. Pavlov was a scientist who had a dog. He set up an experiment where he would ring a bell every time he served it food. The bell became a cue that food was coming, and the dog drooled as a result. Even when Pavlov stopped giving the dog food and only rang the bell, it continued to drool, as it still expected the food. This could be what's going on inside us when we take a pill that we think will work. In expecting an outcome, our brain rationalizes that it will happen.

How our body responds to the placebo can also depend on a variety of factors. The size, shape, color, and number of pills have been shown to make a difference, and injections seem to have an even greater effect than pills. Sometimes even a physician's enthusiasm can trigger the placebo effect. If your doctor is adamant and tells you that something works, you're likely to expect it will.

It can also be hard to keep up with all the placebos out there today because new ones pop up all the time. Magnet therapy, cold vitamins, diet pills, homeopathic medicine, negative ion bracelets, aromatherapy, crystals, and several other things are considered placebos. When there's no scientific evidence that a treatment works but people insist it does, it is likely a result of the placebo effect.

Does this mean that people who wear ion bracelets, do acupuncture, or use homeopathy should stop completely? Not necessarily. Even if these treatments are a placebo, they can have some value. Studies have shown a placebo can increase the endorphins in the brain. This shows our thoughts may actually change our brain chemistry.

We don't need to be ashamed, but we should be aware of what treatments are scientifically proven and what treatments are unproven. Through this, we can be conscious of whether or not the treatment is a placebo and if the cost, time, and energy are worth it.

Lastly, it's also important to realize that while powerful, the placebo effect has its limitations. It can't affect things like heart disease, tumors, broken bones, or viruses.

The placebo effect happens when:

- Person A is presented with a solution that is said to work.

- Person A uses that solution and feels the benefits even though there is no scientific reason for the effectiveness.

An Example with Ethan and Emily

Emily ran down the dock as she held onto the rope attached to the big oak. At the end of the pier, she pulled herself up and swung out over the water. As she reached the end of the arc, she let go, allowing the motion to carry her through the air.

"Yaaaaa," she screamed only seconds before she splashed into the lake. The water enveloped her, and she looked around as little fish swam by her. One tickled her nose, and she smiled before swimming back to the surface where the sun shined brightly overhead.

Breaking the surface, she took in a deep breath and looked back at the dock as her cousin Charlie grabbed hold of the rope. He pulled it back and wrapped it around his arm before taking off with a running start toward the water. He wasn't as graceful as Emily, and as he swung out, he was unable to unwrap it from his arm. His eyes widened as he swung back toward the dock and crashed into it, screaming out in pain.

Emily swam back toward the dock, getting there just before Ethan as Charlie groaned and lay on the dock holding his side.

Emily could see a bruise just above his hip already forming as it darkened and began to swell. She moved her fingers over it. "It's pretty swollen, but hopefully it isn't broken."

"What happened?!" Emily and Ethan's other cousin Darwin yelled as he ran down the dock.

"Charlie didn't let go of the rope and slammed back into the dock," Ethan said.

Darwin pulled a necklace out of his shirt and put it over Charlie's head. "Relax, breathe deep. Feel the power of the crystal."

Emily glanced at Ethan and then back to Charlie. "What is that?" she asked, looking at a red crystal attached to the end of the necklace.

Darwin held the crystal in his hand. "It's red calcite. It's a special healing crystal."

Emily scratched her head. "How can a crystal heal someone?"

Darwin laid the crystal back on Charlie. "I don't know. I think it has something to do with the ions in the atmosphere or the neutrinos in your blood. It doesn't matter. All I know is that it works. Every time I get a headache and I put the crystal around my neck, it gets better within a few minutes."

"That sounds crazy," Ethan said.

Darwin nodded. "It does, but it works."

Ethan shook his head. "There's no way that works."

"If you don't believe me, then ask Charlie." Darwin turned to Charlie.

"Well," Emily asked. "How do you feel?"

Charlie bit his lower lip. "I… It's not as bad as it was. It's getting better." He smiled and sat up. "I think the crystal is working."

"See?" Darwin said. "I told you it works."

What Happened?

When Darwin used the crystal, he felt better because of the placebo effect. In time, his headache naturally went away, but he attributed it to the crystal. When Darwin told Charlie that the crystal healed him, Charlie also started to believe it could remove his pain.

The crystal did absolutely nothing, but as time progressed, the pain subsided, Charlie's brain released endorphins, and he started to feel better. This caused Charlie to mistakenly believe the crystal was effective.

Tuttle Twins Takeaway

We need to let go of our pride and realize that the placebo effect applies to everyone. If we find ourselves using a placebo, it doesn't mean we're foolish, only that our thoughts impact how we perceive a remedy's effectiveness.

If you find yourself using a treatment that isn't scientifically proven, consider it could likely be a placebo. Though placebos are relatively harmless, some may be expensive, time-consuming, or have side effects. If this is the scenario you find yourself in, do some research, consult a qualified physician, and consider their expertise before investing more time and money in any treatments.

BYSTANDER EFFECT

Our brains sometimes shut down during an emergency in a public place, thinking that someone else will provide help. In a group situation, you need to maintain self-awareness.

I'm Not a Doctor

When somebody is in danger, our chance of helping lessens when we're in a crowd. Sometimes, we might fail to help altogether, or we might delay helping. Both can prove deadly in a life-threatening situation. A natural disaster, car accident, fight, crime, or bullying can catch us all off guard. You would assume people would get more help in a crowd than one-on-one, but that's not the case. Why does this happen? There are a few different reasons.

One reason is something called the diffusion of responsibility. Most people assume that somebody else in the group will help the person in trouble. We tell ourselves it's not our responsibility. There are plenty of other people around who can help. They should be the ones to do something. Statements like these help take the burden off us and place it on others. We believe somebody else should take charge, not us.

Another mistake we might make is to assume that somebody else is far better qualified to handle an emergency. We might feel that we don't have the necessary medical or emergency training. Wouldn't somebody more qualified do a better job? If we were to step in, would we make it worse? When we get stuck waiting for someone better to come along, we miss the fact that we might be the most qualified person there. All we're doing by waiting is allowing the situation to worsen.

Fear is another big reason. When no one acts, we fear that we might be misreading the situation. We assume that other people are failing to help because there's no need for it. Even though we feel the correct thing to do would be to help, we convince ourselves it's wrong. We second-guess ourselves as we fear making a mistake (e.g., offering un-wanted or unneeded help, looking silly). Instead of assist-ing someone who needs help, we freeze.

Though we don't like to admit it, selfishness can play a role too. Our own plans are often our main concern. It's hard to admit this, but we justify it in our heads by telling ourselves the situation isn't as bad as it seems. Once we convince ourselves that's the case, then we can rationalize all the rest of our excuses. Essentially, we give ourselves a reason to move on with our lives without any interruption to our plans.

How do we overcome this bias? Recognize that this affects everyone in a crowd. Then forget about what others are doing and ask yourself what you would be doing if you were alone. Would you help the person in need, or would you do nothing? Would it be better to offer help that isn't wanted or not offer help and learn later that you should have? If your gut instinct tells you that someone is in dan-ger, your intuition is usually correct. Yet, that doesn't mean you should put yourself in a dangerous situation either. Make sure that when you find ways to help someone, you do it safely.

If you happen to be the person in trouble and others are paralyzed by the bystander effect, then try singling out one person. Make eye contact with them and ask for help. When confronted directly, it's harder for someone to stand by and do nothing than when they're lost among the crowd.

The bystander effect takes place when:

- Person A is in a crowd and sees Person B is possibly in danger.

- Person A notices no one else is doing anything to help.
- Person A figures their instinct to help is wrong and ignores it.

An Example with Ethan and Emily

Emily and Ethan picked up their gloves and walked away from the baseball field with Kyle and Stacy as their other team members walked with their moms and dads toward the parking lot. Yet, something didn't feel right. As Ethan looked across the park, he saw a man lying in an awkward position at the far end of the field. His one arm was out-stretched, and the other seemed pinned underneath his body. It was hard to see his face.

"Is that guy okay?" Ethan asked.

Stacy looked up. "It's just some guy sleeping."

"Yeah, he is probably homeless or something," Kyle said.

Emily looked in another section of the park and saw a dog on a leash running around. "Whose dog is that? Do you think it belongs to that guy?"

Stacy shook her head back and forth. "Don't bother him. Kyle is probably right. He's homeless, or he could be a drug person," she whispered.

Ethan looked at Emily, Kyle, and Stacy. "We should go check to see if he's hurt."

Kyle and Stacy both stepped back.

"There's a lot of people in this park," Kyle said. "No one else is doing anything. It's not our responsibility to check on everyone who's resting in the park."

"Yeah," said Stacy. "Stop making a big deal out of nothing. He's fine."

Ethan and Emily looked at each other. "Come on," Emily said. "Let's go."

As they ran toward the man in the park, the dog raced up to them. It seemed friendly and ran with them toward the man. When they reached him, they found him awake but incoherent. A phone and bottle of prescription pills lay next to him.

"Are you okay?" Ethan asked.

The man nodded his head and pointed at the pills. Ethan picked them up and read the label. "It's heart medicine. Did you have a heart attack?"

The man mumbled and nodded. Emily picked up his phone and began to dial 911. "It's okay, sir. I'll call an ambulance, and we'll stay with you until they come."

The dog lay down beside him, and Emily and Ethan looked at their friends frozen in the distance. What had caused them to freeze up like that? If Ethan and Emily had listened to them, would anyone have come to help?

What Happened?

Kyle and Stacy didn't want to get involved. They were afraid that they would be offering unwanted help, or even that the person may be an addict and harmful to them. Kyle also insinuated that it wasn't their responsibility to help. It's typical for us to rationalize many different reasons not to do something in a life-threatening situation.

However, Emily and Ethan didn't allow the bystander effect to keep them from coming to the man's aid. They decided to take the risk of offering unwanted help rather than wave it off and regret later that they hadn't done something. In the end, they were glad that they took charge and didn't let the bystander effect get the best of them.

Tuttle Twins Takeaway

When we come across an emergency, we might feel like we should act but freeze up if no one else is doing anything. Don't allow a crowd or group to let you lose your sense of personal responsibility.

Be self-aware, reflect on the emergency, and instead of assuming that everybody is doing what's right, realize that the bystander effect might be affecting them too. Be willing to be the one to help or call for help. It's better to take the risk of investigating a situation to see if someone needs aid than it is to do nothing. With this in mind, we shouldn't place ourselves in danger or perform medical procedures we don't understand. Sometimes the best thing you can do is to alert emergency personnel and wait.

Lastly, if you find yourself in trouble among a crowd, single someone out, make eye contact, and ask for help. You have more chance of getting a response when you address someone directly than when you address the general crowd.

DISOBEY YOUR REASONING WITH

REACTANCE

When someone pressures you to do something, you might find yourself wanting to do the opposite just to resist conforming to what others want.

You're Not My Boss!

Reactance is essentially our gut instinct to rebel when our freedoms are compromised. Instead of listening to authorities' advice, laws, rules, or regulations, we may do the exact opposite of what's demanded as we try to reclaim our freedom.

For instance, when the seat belt laws first came into effect, it was more common to disobey them because of reactance. People had grown up without these laws in place, and many believed they restricted their liberty. Only a fraction of people wore them before the laws, and many refused to obey the new rules—some even went as far as cutting them out of their cars. Over time, though, as people grew up with these laws in place and understood that the benefits outweighed the cost, they were less likely to be reactive, and lives were saved.

Reactance has also changed the course of history. The Boston Tea Party is an excellent example of it. In protest of unfair tax laws, colonists in America threw an entire shipment of tea from the East India Company into the Boston Harbor. The consequences of this weren't favorable to the colonists due to the closing of Boston harbor and institution of the Intolerable Acts, but this was a crucial turning point in the American Revolution. It would one day lead to independence from the crown and the creation of the United States of America.

While it would seem that reactance can protect or promote freedom, it can also destroy it. Some groups have used propaganda to make the general population believe that their liberty was being taken away by some other powerful group. They encouraged reactance (i.e., rebellion) as a way to leverage power for themselves. They championed their group as a means for fighting against a perceived loss of liberty or an injustice. Unfortunately, when these groups gained control, then they were even worse than their predecessors.

Freedom is hard to win and easy to lose. While we should never take it for granted, we also must not allow ourselves to be manipulated or ruled by our emotions. When we do, it can have unintended consequences and even backfire on us. Though reactance may seem like the perfect antidote when our freedoms are impinged upon, that isn't necessarily the case. Take time to think clearly and consider the full effect of the restriction or order. Why do you oppose it? Is it unreasonable or immoral, or is it because you don't like someone telling you what to do? If it's excessive or immoral, how can you react responsibly without hostility?

Reactance consists of:

- Person A has a freedom.

- An authority requests Person A submit to a new rule or restriction that impinges on that freedom.

- Person A does the opposite of what is asked or rebels against the order.

An Example with Ethan and Emily

Ethan and Emily's mom pulled into their neighbor's driveway and put her car into park. She turned around to Ethan and Emily, sitting in the backseat. "I'll only be a moment. I need to drop off this food." She popped open the driver's door, grabbed two giant Tupperware containers from the passenger's seat, and slid out of the car. Walking up to their neighbor's door, a woman opened it and ushered her inside. A moment later, the door closed.

"Why is she bringing meals to our neighbors?" Emily asked.

"I think Mr. Franklin lost his job, and they're not doing too well financially," Ethan said. He looked out the window. His friend Don waited for the bus by the curb, and Ethan popped open his car door.

"Where are you going?" Emily asked.

"I'm going to say hi to Don while we're waiting for Mom. We have at least fifteen minutes, maybe more. You know how she is when she gets talking."

Emily popped open her door and followed Ethan as he approached Don. Their friend was in a new school uniform and didn't look particularly happy.

"How's it going?" Ethan asked.

Don grabbed his uniform collar and tugged on it. "Can you believe this? They're forcing us to wear these. What is this, the Soviet Union?"

"They didn't ask the parents for any input?" Ethan asked.

Don rolled his eyes and shook his head. "The parents voted for it, but it doesn't matter. What we wear should be our decision, not the school board's or our parents'. We aren't babies!" Don stomped his foot.

"Hey," Emily said, "I probably wouldn't be happy about it either, but you should calm down. No use in getting too upset."

Don kicked a piece of sod out of the lawn. "I'm not going to calm down. I'm not going to stand by and let them trample on my freedoms!"

Ethan raised his hands as he tried to calm Don. "It stinks, Don. But there are many worse things in the world than school uniforms, and there are some pluses. You don't have to worry about what you're going to wear in the morning. It saves time, kids have less chance of getting picked on, and it looks professional. Keep it in perspective."

Don glared at Ethan and stuck a finger in his face. "I don't care what they tell me to do. I'll never be professional." He lifted his shirt to reveal what looked like camouflaged pajamas underneath.

"Why are you wearing those?" Emily asked.

Don grinned. "If they think they can push this guy around, then they have another thing coming. I'm changing as soon as I get to school. They can't stop me from expressing myself. It's my First Amendment right."

The bus screeched to a stop alongside them, and Don got on. As it pulled away, Emily and Ethan looked back at their mom's car, trying to figure everything out.

"What was that about?" Emily asked.

"I don't know. I guess Don doesn't like uniforms," Ethan said.

What Happened?

Don didn't like the idea of having to wear school uniforms. He felt like it took away his freedom. Ethan and Emily could understand how he felt. Emily stated she wouldn't like the idea of having to wear uniforms either. Ethan even tried to tell Don some of the benefits he might not have realized about school uniforms.

Don didn't care, however, and he couldn't get beyond his emotions. He wasn't able to allow himself to reflect on the big picture. All he could focus on was that someone wanted him to wear something that he didn't want to wear. In response, he got upset and declared he would never follow the rule. He even went as far as preparing to change into his pajamas to protest the new dress code.

Tuttle Twins Takeaway

When you find yourself wanting to act out because of a loss of personal freedom, take some time to reflect on the situation. Are you allowing your emotions to lead you instead of thinking clearly? By relying on your feelings as the primary justification for your actions, you may end up making poor decisions. Before you react, ask yourself why the restriction was implemented, get outside feedback, and weigh its pros and cons.

Nevertheless, sometimes it's appropriate to push back against restrictions. We live in the world we do thanks to those who dared to stand up against injustice. If we don't act to protect our liberties, then who will? Again, freedom is something that's hard to win and easy to lose. And as

Benjamin Franklin once said, "Those that can give up essential liberty to gain a little temporary safety deserve neither liberty nor safety."

SPOTLIGHT EFFECT

You probably think that others notice you more than they actually do. Most people are more concerned with themselves than they are about you.

Everyone is Watching

Our problem is that we're the center of our universe. We put an inordinate amount of importance on how we look and what we say. If our hair sticks up, we have a pimple, or we say something dumb, we might think everybody notices. When we mess up in a recital, play, or game, it seems like the end of the world. We believe everyone notices or remembers everything about us. As a result, we might feel scrutinized, become overly self-conscious, or dread social situations.

This might be because someone commented on our flaws once, and now we assume that everyone obsesses about them. They don't. It's only in our heads that this delusion exists. While it's good to examine ourselves from time to time, it's not good to obsess. Obsession means we're so focused on something that we forget about everything else. We're not present and fully aware in the moment. We don't think about others and what they're going through and miss opportunities to help them. Our ego gets in the way and stops us from positively impacting the world by serving others.

Don't believe it? Can you remember what your friends were wearing at the beginning of the week? How was their hair styled? Did they say anything dumb? If you can't, you might assume that's because they don't have flaws, but that's not true. It's just that you're not paying that much attention. If you can't remember this about your friends, then what about your acquaintances? Maybe a few things stick out, but you miss a lot because you're self-centered, just like everyone else.

An excellent way to get out of this bias is by focusing our attention on others instead of ourselves. What do their expressions and body language tell you? How do they feel? What might be bothering them, or what might they be excited about? Try to make a game out of learning something new about others each day. Look for clues. Show them that you value them and what they have to say.

Another exercise you could do to put things in perspective is to ask yourself a would-you-rather question. Would you rather be friends with someone who has perfect hair and clothes but doesn't listen to a word you say, or someone who listens to you and is eager to learn more about you but has a bad haircut and a stain on their shirt? We probably can all remember when someone screwed something up or didn't look their best, but those things fade away over time and aren't important. Don't allow the unimportant parts of life (e.g., how you look or act) let you lose sight of the important people who surround you and how you can make a deep and meaningful impact on their lives.

The spotlight effect happens when:

- Person A fixates on their appearance or behavior.

- Person A believes others also fixate on Person A's appearance or behavior.

An Example with Ethan and Emily

Emily, Ethan, and several of their friends walked along the edge of the park with orange vests on and garbage bags in hand. The park was a mess, and they were on the Teen Volunteer Cleanup Crew. Once a month, they would get together and tackle a different challenge. This month, it was picking up litter in one of the more neglected public parks.

The month before, it was cleaning up graffiti in another part of the city.

Emily picked up an old wrapper with her litter stick and dropped it into a garbage bag as Ethan found a can.

"Oh, five more cents. I'm getting close to that bike." Ethan smiled.

Emily smiled back. "Nice job, only three-thousand-nine-hundred-and-ninety-five cans to go."

All the kids spread out around the park, slowly filling their bags. As Ethan reached for another can, he heard Emily sneeze.

"God bless you, Emily."

"I didn't sneeze."

Ethan looked up. All the other kids were several yards away. The only one within a few feet of him was Emily. They looked at each other confused. Suddenly, someone sneezed again. It was coming from the bushes right next to Emily.

Ethan peered through the undergrowth. "Is someone in there?"

"Leave me alone," said a girl's voice.

"Lucy?" Emily asked. "What are you doing in there? Aren't you supposed to be helping us clean up?"

"I can't let anyone see me like this. It's horrible. I'm just going to wait in here for the rest of the day until it's dark."

Emily and Ethan looked at each other. "Come on," said Emily. "You can't stay in there all day."

"Yes, I can."

"Come out. I promise we won't laugh. Whatever it is, it can't be that bad," said Ethan as he imagined the worst and gritted his teeth.

The bushes rustled as Lucy slid her way out the back and peeked around the corner. "Is anyone else out there?"

Emily looked behind her. "Just a few others, but they're busy picking up trash."

Lucy retreated behind the bush. "I can't let them see me. You'll have to come here."

Ethan shrugged his shoulders, and he and Emily made their way around the back of the bush. When they found Lucy, she was wearing some jeans, a T-shirt, and an orange vest. They looked her up and down. Her sneakers looked okay. There were no stains or problems with her clothing, and her hair seemed fine. She had no blemishes or anything like that. The only thing was her eyes were a little puffy from crying. As she looked at Emily and Ethan, she began to retreat into the bush before Emily grabbed hold of her wrist and stopped her.

"What's wrong, Lucy?"

"Don't pretend you don't know. It's awful. I told my mom not to make me come, but she wouldn't listen. Everyone's going to think I'm the biggest loser in the world."

"What are you talking about?" Ethan asked.

"This," Lucy said as she pulled at her hair.

"I don't understand," Emily said.

Lucy held back tears. "Stop humoring me. I look like a clown."

Ethan looked closer. He could see a very light green tint to some strands of her hair if the light hit it just right. "The green?"

Lucy began to sob. "My mom gave me highlights, and I went in the pool. When I came out, it had turned green. Everyone's going to laugh at me."

Emily put her hand on her shoulder. "Lucy, no one's going to notice. You can barely see it, and even if someone does, they won't care. They'll probably think you did it on purpose."

Lucy sniffed. "You're just saying that to make me feel better."

"Look at me, Lucy. Would I lie?"

Ethan held out his hand. Lucy took it and stepped out of the bushes as she looked around at the other kids.

"Come on," said Emily. "Let's clean up the park."

Emily, Ethan, and Lucy made their way around the park. They interacted with several other kids, and to Lucy's surprise, not a single person said a thing about her hair.

What Happened?

We all spend an inordinate amount of time focused on our appearance and how we act compared to others. Each of us is the center of our own universe. For Lucy, she believed that how she saw the world was the same way everyone else did—with Lucy at the center. This made her extremely self-conscious. She thought everyone noticed her every flaw and mistake and cared about it.

If she asked herself if she remembered other people's hair issues, she would have realized she'd have a hard time recalling any. In this, she would have understood that the attention on her was far less than she had previously thought. Her appearance and behaviors weren't as significant as she made them out to be, just like everyone else's.

Tuttle Twins Takeaway

We can be so focused on ourselves that we assume everyone else is focused on us too. They aren't. It's not because they don't care about us, but because we're just one out of dozens of others they come into contact with daily. Even in our small circles, no one else has the time or energy to pay attention to everyone as much as they do to themselves.

When you're feeling self-conscious or worried about how you look or something you did, transfer the flaw to someone else. Would you notice it if they weren't you? Do you remember all the pimples, stray hairs, and shirt stains of your best friend or the silly things they said? Even if you do remember something, does that change your opinion of them?

Also, instead of focusing on what you feel are your inadequacies, think about others. What excites them or what might be bothering them? Make it a game of learning something new about others each day. If you can realize the world isn't centered around you, it will not only make life easier, but you'll also have more enjoyment as you find ways to make the world a better place.

So, what did you think? (Get it?)

We covered a lot of material, and it's important that you revisit this book periodically so that you can keep these ideas fresh in your mind. We tend to forget over time, and you'll want to review and remember.

Have you heard how many adults say that when they buy a certain car, suddenly they see that car everywhere? Perhaps you've experienced this with a certain article of clothing. When we have a direct connection to something, we tend to notice it more when we see it elsewhere.

It's the same with these cognitive biases. Now that you know a bit more about each of them, you're going to start noticing them more often in others. Perhaps you'll see one used by a movie character, a friend, or a sibling.

And more importantly, you'll start to better notice how you are using them yourself. Having read this book, you'll more clearly be able to think through if and how you're thinking poorly, and avoid these biases in the future.

We're excited to see how you use this information in your life. Share these ideas with your family and kindly point out biases when you see them. That way, everyone can learn together and talk through how we can improve our communication and better pursue the truth!

—The Tuttle Twins